Lucrative Practices

The Comprehensive Handbook for Healthcare Executives

By Michael B. Spellman, Ph.D.

American Association for
PHYSICIAN
LEADERSHIP

PUBLISHER
Nancy Collins

EDITORIAL ASSISTANT
Jennifer Weiss

DESIGN & LAYOUT
Carter Publishing Studio

COPYEDITOR
Pat George

In loving memory of
Matthew Harold Spellman

Table of Contents

LIST OF FIGURES

INDEX OF ACRONYMS

DAP	Disciplinary Action Plan
DEA	Drug Enforcement Agency
DoL	U.S. Department of Labor
EBDITA	Earnings Before, Depreciation, Interest, Taxes, and Amortization
EFTPS	Electronic Federal Tax Payment System
EFT	Electronic Funds Transfer
EHR	Electronic Health Record
EMR	Electronic Medical Record
ERA	Electronic Remittance Advice
ERA	Electronic Remittance Advisory
EBSA	Employee Benefits Security Administration
ERISA	Employee Retirement Income Security Act of 1974
EIN	Employer Identification Number
ERN	Employer Registration Number
E/M	Evaluation and Management codes
EPO	Exclusive Provider Organization
EOB	Explanation of Benefits
FDCPA	Fair Debt Collection Practices Act of 1977
FLSA	Fair Labor Standards Act of 1938
FCA	False Claims Act of 1863
FICA	Federal Insurance Contributions Act
FTC	Federal Trade Commission
FUTA	Federal Unemployment Tax
FFS	Fee-For-Service
FF&E	Furniture, Fixtures, and Equipment
HHS	U.S. Department of Health and Human Services
HIE	Health Information Exchange
HITECH	Health Information Technology for Economic and Clinical Health Act

HIPAA	Health Insurance Portability and Accountability Act of 1996
HMO	Health Maintenance Organization
HCPCS	Healthcare Common Procedure Coding System
HCFA	Health Care Financing Administration
IRA	Individual Retirement Account
IM	Instant Messaging
IRS	Internal Revenue Service
ICD	International Classification of Diseases and Related Health Problems
ISP	Internet Service Provider
LOP	Letter of Protection
LOC	Line of Credit
MCO	Managed Care Organization
MACRA	Medicare Access and CHIP Reauthorization Act of 2015
MACs	Medicare Administrative Contractors
MSPB	Medicare Spending Per Beneficiary
MIPS	Merit-Based Incentive Payment System
NPPES	National Plan and Provider Enumeration System
NPI	National Provider Identifier
NPP	Notice of Privacy Practices
OSHA	Occupational Safety and Health Act of 1970
OCR	Office of Civil Rights
OA	Other Adjustment
PI	Payer Initiated Reduction
PHR	Personal Health Record
POA	Power of Attorney
PPO	Preferred Provider Organization
PCAP	Progressive Corrective Action Plan
PHI	Protected Health Information

PECOS   Provider Enrollment, Chain, and Ownership System

PTAN   Provider Transaction Access Number

RVU   Relative Value Units

ROI   Return On Investment

SECA   Self-Employment Compensation Taxes

SEP   Simplified Employee Pension IRA

SCA   Single Case Agreement

SPS   Single-Payer System

SNF   Skilled Nursing Facility

SSN   Social Security Number

TAT   Tangible Assets Tax

TIN   Taxpayer Identification Number

UPIN   Unique Physician Identification Number

UR   Utilization Review

VBP   Value-Based Payment

VA   Veterans Administration

VOIP   Voice-Over-Internet Protocol

WHO   World Health Organization

Acknowledgments

Book writing and business management have some things in common. For example, CEOs typically get the credit for a business' successes; in writing, the credit goes to the author. However, neither the CEO nor the author could have accomplished their goals without the support of others. Although I penned the words, the ideas for this book came from decades of consulting with clients who graciously invited me into their businesses and practices. Their willingness to openly share their problems, their successes and their management styles provided me with an education like no other. I am grateful to each of them for the education they provided and for entrusting me with their business affairs and their aspirations.

Success in business and in writing also require access to, and openness to, honest critique. I am particularly grateful to all of those friends, colleagues, and sometimes strangers who took the time to read early drafts of this book and to share their thoughts about how each draft could be improved. Fortunately, even the harshest critics were also able and willing to share what they liked and found helpful in the book. Some, like my wife Dr. Debra Carter, were both my harshest critics and my most enthusiastic cheerleaders. Thank you, all.

Many businesses and certainly publishing have people working in the background whose input and support are invaluable. Thank you, Nancy Collins, Patricia George, and the staff of AAPL for your guidance and support through this painstaking process.

About the Author

MICHAEL SPELLMAN is a healthcare practice consultant with more than 30 years of experience in a wide range of healthcare practice types and settings. He is fond of saying that "Practice consultancy provides the best possible education. Where else can you learn from other's successes and from their mistakes?"

Dr. Spellman is a clinician and entrepreneur who knows firsthand what it takes to be successful as a healthcare professional starting, running, and ultimately selling healthcare businesses of all sizes.

A licensed psychologist who continues to practice part-time, he adds an understanding of human motivations and human behaviors to his work. His experiences as a member of Florida's Commission on Mental Health and Substance Abuse and as the longstanding chairman of a political action committee help Dr. Spellman understand and use the political, regulatory, economic, and social forces that influence the healthcare industry.

A frequent speaker on the topic of The Business of Practice, Dr. Spellman consults to practices and facilities of all sizes. Topics and services of interest to healthcare entrepreneurs can be found at: LucrativePractices.com

Dr. Spellman enjoys traveling with his wife, Dr. Debra Carter, herself an author.

Becoming a Healthcare Entrepreneur

Professionals from every healthcare profession can successfully apply the principles of entrepreneurship to their businesses. Properly trained managers and support staff can increase their value to their employer by learning and helping to implement these same principles. Regardless of whether you are a current practice owner, an aspiring owner, a manager, or a support staff member, you can adapt qualities, perspectives, and ways of thinking to become a successful Healthcare Entrepreneur.

As a Healthcare Entrepreneur, you must expand how you think about your practice. This means adding a business dimension to your perspective, all the while pursuing your dreams, goals, and aspirations. Healthcare Entrepreneurs structure their businesses to maximize lifetime earnings; therefore, the primary financial metric is "What is the value of my company?"

Certainly, money is a part of your business's value, but esoteric values such as quality of care also must be taken into account. Looking only at the money or only at the more personal values diminishes both. Attending to both enhances both.

When applied thoughtfully, the best business models in healthcare also result in the highest possible quality of care. In fact, failure to implement the principles of Healthcare Entrepreneurship can actually diminish the quality of care. An example comes from the professionals who must limit their time spent with each patient in order to see enough patients to make ends meet. Healthcare Entrepreneurs use business principles to remain profitable without having to cut clinically valuable corners or sacrifice job satisfaction.

Making the shift from traditional thinking to Healthcare Entrepreneurship thinking requires an ongoing commitment. Ingrained habits and the historical sociologic tenets of most professions may act as inhibiting forces. Fear of censure by your peers for opening new paths can compete with your desire to succeed. In reality, there is nothing to fear. Successful Healthcare Entrepreneurs tend to be admired by their peers and sought after by their patients.

As a Healthcare Entrepreneur, you will recognize that the business you own has value. How that value benefits you and increases your personal wealth depends on the decisions you make. Certainly, the salary, dividends, and bonuses you draw from the business are among the benefits. They are not the only considerations, however. Nor are they the primary considerations driving decisions. For example, as a Healthcare Entrepreneur, you may choose to take home less money in any given year so you can invest in equipment that will make a larger contribution to your personal wealth at a later time.

> *"A decent hockey player always knows where the puck is.*
> *Great hockey players know where the puck is going to be."*
> *— Wayne Gretzky*

This does not mean Healthcare Entrepreneurs ignore their annual profits; they keep their eyes on both their current profits and on the value of their business. Healthcare Entrepreneurs make business decisions by determining how their decision will affect the monetary value of the business over the near term and the long term. For example, consider a physician who has an option to purchase an expensive piece of diagnostic equipment. Over the near term, the cost of doing so will diminish net profits. Over the longer term, however, owning that equipment will likely bring in more patients, resulting in more profitable billings per patient and increasing the value of the business when it comes time to sell. All other factors being equal, the savvy Healthcare Entrepreneur likely will invest in the future and purchase the equipment.

Unlike business owners in other industries, far too many healthcare practitioners simply shutter a practice when they are ready to leave or sell the practice to a colleague at a price well below its true value. Healthcare Entrepreneurs are always tracking the value of their business and building that value. When the time comes to sell their business, they are in a position to profit and, in a very real way, keep profiting personally long after they have retired.

The healthcare industry is fraught with risks. Although some people choose to avoid thinking about them, no one in any business is immune from risks. Healthcare Entrepreneurs manage and master their risks by staying on top of the information flow regarding factors that impact their business and by making informed decisions. Likewise, they know their own level of risk tolerance and make decisions commensurate with that level.

There are no right or wrong levels of risk tolerance for a Healthcare Entrepreneur. For example, some adhere to conservative operating models; they will not enter a new market, offer a new service, experiment with new technology, or take other risks until the new market, service, or technology has proven itself. This approach reduces the risks but also tends to reduce the rewards. Other Healthcare Entrepreneurs follow an "early adopter" model. These professionals keep their eyes on future trends and consider the predictor variables that might help them "get a jump on" new trends that turn into profitable options. They maximize profits by staying ahead of the curve.

There is one exception to the "no right or wrong" principle of risk-taking in the business world: impulsivity. Certainly, there are Healthcare Entrepreneurs who tell tantalizing stories of a profitable decision made purely on intuition. Their success is a product of chance; if you roll the dice often enough, eventually, you will come up with snake eyes. Successful Healthcare Entrepreneurs know to walk away from the table when they experience such a fortunate gain. It is foolhardy to take the profits from random good fortune and re-invest them impulsively in another risky venture. Owning a successful business is hard work, and much of that work involves learning about, understanding, and keeping on top of the information that guides productive business decisions.

In the tumultuous world of healthcare, Healthcare Entrepreneurs learn to manage and adapt to change. More often than not, they choose to make changes rather than feeling compelled to change in reaction to outside forces. Healthcare Entrepreneurs think outside the box and develop profitable opportunities within the boundaries of their circumstances. For example, when faced with fee cuts in excess of 50%, an entrepreneurially minded Ophthalmology group, recognizing that most of their patients were senior citizens with the predictable health needs associated with late life, added audiology, dermatology, and a balance clinic to their business. Everyone benefited; the patients had easy access to oft-needed services, and the practice limited the negative financial impact of the fee reductions.

Healthcare Entrepreneurs are open to re-inventing their businesses to take advantage of new opportunities. Traditional practitioners, on the other hand, tend to have a narrowly defined range of activities in which they can and will engage. Healthcare professionals offer a striking number of explanations when asked why they did not take advantage of new opportunities or why they did not make minor changes to increase profitability. Too often, the explanation is simply, "I never thought of that."

Not all Healthcare Entrepreneurs are practice owners. Those who work with, and sometimes for, others are called Intrapreneurs, reflecting the fact that they bring their entrepreneurial skills and spirit IN to other organizations. Some examples of Intrapreneurs are Office Managers, Contracted Managers, and Practice Consultants. Intrapreneurs are professionals who set up or manage entrepreneurial projects in partnership with or on behalf of a company they do not own.

TIP: 50% of a lot can often be more than 100% of a little.

Successful Intrapreneurs must have the skills needed to create a business independently, along with the skills required to successfully navigate the politics of a larger organization. Those who bring both to the table can create lucrative opportunities. For example, consider the Physical Therapist who is contemplating opening a second office in a nearby town that does not currently have access to physical therapy services. One option is for the Physical Therapist to take all the risk and open a satellite office. Another option might be to negotiate with the local hospital to open a physical therapy department as a joint venture. With the entrepreneurial Physical Therapist at the helm, the risks and profits are shared. There is room for everyone to gain.

YOUR VISION

You can take the first step in building a practice from virtually anywhere in the world. Write down your vision for the practice, first describing the big picture and then giving it substance by including as much detail as your imagination will allow. This may sound simpler than it is; moving ideas into plans and wishful plans into actionable plans can be challenging. A person who is genuinely committed to having a successful practice most likely will have already spent time daydreaming about the future, but now is the time to go beyond the passive stage of fantasizing.

Once you have written down your daydreams, consider them from different angles. Talk to friends and mentors to learn their thoughts. Begin to write down, in clear, concrete terms, what it will take to convert your dreams into reality. Most aspects of business should be viewed as a ratio, so in addition to considering the potentials of your ideas, also consider the costs and risks. Likewise, most things in business happen in steps and stages. Think through the steps and stages and write those down as well. With these few steps, you have begun to write a business plan.

CASE STUDY

Business Planning

Dr. Iris Jones had been formulating her dream plastic surgery practice before she was even accepted to medical school. She knew from an early age that she wanted to be a Plastic Surgeon and had no doubts that she would be accepted into and successfully complete the requisite training. For this reason, early in life, she sought and secured a job in a local plastic surgery practice. There she worked as a Receptionist on both the medical side and the retail spa side of the practice. She learned a lot about what it takes to operate a successful practice.

Moreover, she was able to think through alternative ways to improve the practice at which she was employed. She kept notes of her ideas and updated those notes throughout her professional training. After residency, she was able to convert those notes into a business plan that helped leapfrog her career several steps ahead of her residency cohort.

YOUR BUSINESS PLAN

A business plan is an essential (let me say that again: *essential*) tool for those who want to maximize their success. Experts often cite the lack of a business plan as one of the leading causes of business failure. Savvy investors will not even consider an investment opportunity if it is not backed by a business plan. If savvy businesspeople will not risk investing in a business that lacks a business plan, why should you?

Writing your business plan requires thought, research, and informed decision making. The more fully developed and detailed your business plan is, the better it will serve you. Each section of this book focuses on one of the essential factors you should consider and include in your business plan. The information provided is not exhaustive; each topic is worthy of its own book.

A list of the major headings for a basic business plan is shown in Table 1. There is nothing magical or sacrosanct about the list; you can modify it to fit your needs. Basic business plans guide you toward goals, help you stay on track in meeting those goals, and help you maintain your focus on factors that might enhance or interfere with your business. Keep in mind that banks often require a business plan before they will lend you money.

TABLE 1. Major Headings for a Business Plan

1. Executive Summary
2. Description of the Company (Who, What, When, Where, Why, How)
3. Market Analysis
4. Analysis of Competitors, Challenges, and How They Will Be Addressed
5. Sales and Marketing Plan
6. Management Plan
7. Operating Plan
8. Financial Plan
9. Supporting Documents and Exhibits

Any time you must make a significant business decision, consult your business plan. Once you make a decision, revise the plan to reflect the associated changes. By way of example, consider an internal medicine group that has been approached by a local hospital interested in purchasing the group. The group stands out as an attractive acquisition in part because of its consistent pattern of substantial growth over the past several years. The hospital's offer includes a purchase price that seems low to the principles of the group. A quick review of the business plan will remind them of the factors that promoted their recent successes. The data underlying the plan may predict many more years of growth, in which case the practitioners may choose to pass on the hospital's offer. Alternatively, the plan may point to a slowing trend, in which case the hospital's offer may deserve full consideration. Armed with the information in their business plan, the principals in the group will be better prepared to successfully negotiate a more favorable price and other terms if they do choose to pursue the acquisition.

TIP: Business plans are living documents and as such should be reviewed and updated regularly.

Completing a business plan can sometimes be discouraging to would-be Healthcare Entrepreneurs. Because it is difficult to find the time to finalize the plan when one is completing professional training, it may be necessary to hire a Consultant to write the plan for you. One way or the other, the time or money you invest in a business plan is well worth it.

NAMING YOUR BUSINESS AND CHOOSING A D/B/A

To legally register your business, you must give the business a name. In many jurisdictions, if you register your business as one of the legal entity types discussed below, the name under which you register is protected, and the right to use that name belongs only to you or the company that registered the name. If you choose not to organize your business as a corporate entity, you should still register your business's name with the appropriate authority in your state or jurisdiction.

The name you choose is the name you will be "doing business as." Often referred to simply as your "d/b/a," this is the name you will be marketing and building your business's reputation around. For example, Susan Jones, ARNP, may choose to incorporate as a Professional Association registered as "Susan Jones, ARNP, PA." This becomes the legal name of her company. But, she may also register "ARNPs Where You Need Them" as a d/b/a with which to better communicate the services her locum tenens company provides. In most jurisdictions, registering your d/b/a protects your right to use that name exclusively, thus protecting you from others who may try to capitalize on your success.

TIP: In many jurisdictions, a d/b/a must be renewed. Don't forget to do that.

Healthcare professionals often choose their own personal names and professional credentials as the name for their corporation. For instance, Optometrist Tamara Smith, OD, might name her corporation Tamara Smith, OD, LLC. This is a perfectly acceptable business name that would attract patients who already know that Dr. Smith is a well-educated, skillful Optometrist. It might be confusing, however, for patients who do not know that OD means Doctor of Optometry. Dr. Smith could, therefore, also register and use a more descriptive d/b/a name, such as "20/20 Family Eye Care." This name would attract patients who need an Optometrist but do not know Dr. Smith. Having both names would be a distinct marketing advantage.

Having a descriptive d/b/a name is also advantageous when a practitioner wants to add professional partners to the practice or sell the practice. A descriptive corporate d/b/a is more readily transferrable and will more easily accommodate a new partner or owner. Some of the original owner's professional reputation and goodwill are attached to the d/b/a name. This increases the value and thus the sale price of the business. If the practice is only named for its founder, the name cannot as readily be transferred to a different owner, and the new owner will need to choose a new name.

TIP: Once you have chosen a name or narrowed your options to a short list of potential names, check to ensure the name is available. Most jurisdictions have searchable online databases of names that have already been reserved either as a d/b/a or as the name of a registered corporation.

Even if you are sure a name is not already taken in your local or state jurisdiction, think carefully about whether and how the name may be in use elsewhere. For example, naming a practice Amazon Allergy Group or Dupont Plastic Surgery may be tempting because the names Amazon and Dupont are already familiar to most consumers and may elicit positive associations in prospective patients' minds. However, even though they may not have registered their names in your jurisdiction, Amazon and Dupont may file objections to your use of their brand name. Sometimes a simple internet search can show whether the name you prefer is in use elsewhere in the world.

LEGALLY ORGANIZING YOUR BUSINESS

There are many ways in which you can legally organize your business. The pros and cons of each option vary by jurisdiction and depend on your personal goals and circumstances. Although you can form a business, such as a corporation, inexpensively and fairly easily using the internet, you should seek input from Accountants and Attorneys. Your Attorney and Certified Public Accountant (CPA) will have valuable knowledge about the best type of organization for you. The structure you choose has implications for how you will be taxed and the types of liability protections you will need. The following descriptive summaries address some of the implications associated with each form of organization. Remember, laws vary from jurisdiction to jurisdiction, so always check with an Attorney when starting a business.

Sole Proprietorships

Sole Proprietorship is a straightforward and inexpensive form of unincorporated business structure available to individuals who plan to conduct business without partners or employees. For most practical purposes, the business and the business owner are one and the same. Business profits are reported on the owner's personal tax form rather than on a separate business tax form.

Liabilities arising from the business apply directly to and are the responsibility of the Sole Proprietor. In other words, Sole Proprietorships afford less liability protection than other organizational structures. At the same time, there are no expenses associated with separately insuring a legally organized corporation.

General Partnerships

General Partnership, another unincorporated business model, has some features in common with Sole Proprietorships. In a General Partnership, two or more people combine and share resources, risks, and advantages. Partnership documents should be drawn up in as much detail as possible to reduce the chances that disagreements may emerge later.

As with Sole Proprietorships, the income from a General Partnership is reported on each partner's personal income tax form. Liabilities associated with the business are the direct responsibility of the business owners.

LLCs, PLLCs, PAs, and PCs

Limited Liability Corporations (LLCs), when properly incorporated, organized, and operated, provide the owner or partners with some degree of insulation from liabilities. The LLC is considered to be an entity that is separate from and independent of its owner. Likewise, the owner is considered to be a separate entity independent from the LLC. Therefore, in theory, liabilities attributable to the LLC are the responsibility of the LLC, not the owner. Whether this actually proves to be the case depends on several factors.

Too often, the owner of an LLC, or other corporation, blurs the lines between themselves and the corporation. For example, the owner may use the resources of the LLC as if they were the owner's personal assets. To maximize the benefits of this type of organization, the owner must treat the LLC as a completely separate entity, avoiding traps such as the comingling of funds or failing to convene and document requisite shareholders' meetings.

Some states allow professionals to form an entity known as a Professional Limited Liability Company (PLLC). In addition, many states offer the option of incorporating as a Professional Corporation (PC) or Professional Association (PA). Some states also have unique ways to manage the incorporation of licensed professionals. California, for example, offers its licensed professionals the option of a Registered Limited Liability Partnership (RLLP).

Although these organizational structures vary from state to state, a common attribute is that they are separate from their owners, which in theory provides some form of liability protection. The precise nature of the protection varies by type of entity and from state to state. These protections are supposed to serve as a "corporate shield" to insulate the individual owner from the corporation's liabilities. The shield can be flimsy, so is sometimes referred to as the "corporate veil."

Some types of professional corporations require that all owners be in the same profession. For example, a Physiatrist licensed as a Medical Doctor could become a partner in a PA belonging to an Orthopedist who is also licensed as a Medical Doctor. The same Physiatrist may not be eligible to be a partner in a PA that is owned by a Physical Therapist or other rehabilitation professional. Fortunately, corporate structures can be readily changed when it is necessary or expedient to do so. Thus, the Physical Therapist who wants to bring in a Physiatrist as a partner may choose to change corporate structures from a PA to an LLC or corporation.

Corporations

Terminology can be confusing when it comes to corporate structures and other legally defined concepts. For example, it is appropriate to describe a practice as "incorporated" if it has any of the corporate structures described above. However, a Corporation is a specific type of corporate structure. Commonly referred to as an incorporation and designated by "Inc.," this type of structure is most commonly chosen when the group is made up of different professions and when some of the officers and/or directors may not be owners of the business.

Changes in the healthcare industry portend an increase in the number of companies organizing as an Inc. While absentee and corporate ownership are not new in healthcare, both are becoming more common and are likely to become even more so over time. Likewise, as healthcare professional groups grow larger, more of them will employ executives who will serve as directors or officers of the Corporation without an ownership stake.

Regardless of the type of entity you choose, once the entity is formed, several documents will be required in order for you to conduct business with banks and other entities. Your company will need its own Taxpayer Identification Number (TIN) and Articles of Incorporation, which must be filed with the state agency that regulates corporations in your state. The Articles confirm the formation of the Corporation, how much stock has been issued, and other pertinent facts.

> **TIP:** If you are seeking the protection of a corporate structure, ensure all monies are paid to the corporation, not to you. The company can then pay you as an individual.

Corporate bylaws serve as the constitution for your business. They do not typically include the rules, policies, or procedures by which you will operate; instead, they focus on the authorities and responsibilities of the officers of the Corporation. Keep these documents handy and append them to your business plan.

S-Corps versus C-Corps

Regardless of the type of corporate structure, every business entity that is incorporated in the United States must file its own income tax forms with the Internal Revenue Service (IRS). The IRS recognizes two types of corporations, which are designated by the section of the IRS code under which they were created. Healthcare professionals tend to favor S-Corporations (often referred to as S-Corps).

In practical terms, profits from an S-Corp "flow through" the corporation and straight onto the tax form filed by the owner (IRS Form 1040) without the corporation being separately taxed. This means that, even though the corporation must report its income on a separate form (IRS Form 1120S), the income itself is taxed only once as part of the owner's income.

In contrast, corporations organized as a C-Corporation (C-Corp) file their own tax forms and pay taxes on the corporation's income. The owner's then declare the company's profits on their personal income tax form 1040.

One may wonder why anyone would choose to own a C-Corp. One reason is that the S-Corp structure is available only to entities with fewer than 100 owners. The trend among healthcare groups is to become larger and larger, so the S-Corp isn't always an option. Also, in the Healthcare Entrepreneurial spirit, more and more health-related businesses are set up as publicly traded companies, thus making them ineligible for S-Corp status.

Another reason business owners choose C-Corp status is that there are times when personal income from other sources raises the owner's tax burden to the point that it is financially advantageous to defer accepting additional personal income to a future date. C-Corps can retain cash assets at the end of the tax year — something that is not possible to do in an S-Corp.

At the end of each tax year, profits are drained from S-Corps and credited to the owners. This leaves each owner of an S-Corp with a tax burden. The owners of a C-Corp are not personally taxed on the income retained in their C-Corp until the corporation disburses that income to them. Therefore, leaving available profits in the C-Corp is one option by which owners can reduce taxable personal income.

PERMITS, LICENSES, AND NUMBERS

The kinds of permits, licenses, and registration numbers that professionals must obtain before they can practice independently varies from jurisdiction to jurisdiction. Check with each governing body in your jurisdiction to make sure you are in compliance before opening your business. Several permits, licenses, and registration numbers warrant discussion.

National Provider Identifier Number (NPI)

Everyone in a healthcare profession in the United States must have a National Provider Identifier Number (NPI). This is a requirement of federal law and is one of the components of HIPAA (discussed later in this book). It is not true that only professionals who plan to accept Medicare or Medicaid must have an NPI number.

There is no application fee associated with obtaining an NPI; however, before you can finalize your application, you must decide where you fit into the Healthcare Provider Taxonomy Code Set, which lists many provider types and subtypes. Take the time needed to correctly identify yourself to the National Plan and Provider Enumeration System (NPPES), which oversees the process. For example, if you are a Psychologist (taxonomy code: 103T00000X) you may fail to register to provide psychoanalytic services (taxonomy code: 102L00000X) even though you provide both services and qualify for both code registrations. A good place to start is the website at https://nppes.cms.hhs.gov/NPPES/Welcome.do.

Provider Enrollment, Chain, and Ownership System (PECOS) Registration

Most healthcare professionals must register with the Provider Enrollment, Chain, and Ownership System (PECOS), although it does not issue any permits or licenses. PECOS is an online information-recording system used by professionals who participate in Medicare. Failure to register with PECOS can have negative repercussions, including the denial of claims. Begin registration at https://pecos.cms.hhs.gov/pecos/login.do#headingLv1.

Provider Transaction Access Number (PTAN)

Those who choose to provide services to Medicare beneficiaries must obtain a Provider Transaction Access Number (PTAN). PTANs are issued by the Medicare Administrative Contractors (MACs) in response to enrollment and other applications made by professionals and others to Medicare. The MACs are corporations that manage Medicare business functions. Each state or other region has one or more MACs. It is the local MAC that processes claims and forms such as applications to participate as a Medicare provider, change-of-address forms, and applications to reassign monies paid out for services rendered by an individual to that individual's company or employer.

TIP: Even licensing agencies that accept national examination scores and training documents as proof of competence tend to require applicants to pass tests specific to each state on topics such as laws and regulations. Be prepared to take any required examinations.

The PTAN identifies the person who rendered services and is a reference for anyone gaining access to information, such as the status of an outstanding claim using Medicare's Interactive Voice Response (IVR) phone system.

Unique Physician Identification Number (UPIN)

Unique Physician Identification Numbers (UPINs) are no longer in use. Prior to the conversion to NPI numbers, UPINs were required of many, but not all, healthcare providers who chose to render services as Medicare providers.

Professional Licenses

Most healthcare professions in the United States are regulated at the state level. Therefore, the requirements for obtaining a license vary from state to state. In most states, a regulatory body is assigned to each of the primary health professions. Because the licensing process can take quite a bit of time, it is important to begin the application process as soon as you have decided to practice in a given state. Application fees and renewal fees tend to be steep.

Regulators, including licensing boards, typically operate on the theory that a license to practice a regulated profession is a privilege, not a right. Adjust your business plan to ensure compliance with state and local requirements associated with your license and be prepared to have aspects of your professional and personal conduct placed under the control of the regulatory body.

Drug Enforcement Agency Number

Drug Enforcement Agency (DEA) numbers are *not* required of every healthcare professional; however, those professionals who are licensed to prescribe medications and plan to do so must obtain a DEA number. Required under the Drug Enforcement Act of 1970, DEA numbers come in several categories. For many individuals, Form 224, which is available and can be completed at the DEA website, is sufficient. Professionals who are considering opening a narcotic treatment clinic should consider whether they will need a separate DEA number for the clinic. Fees for DEA numbers are fairly steep, and the numbers must be renewed (and paid for) every three years. Visit the DEA website for an application: https://apps.deadiversion. usdoj.gov/webforms/.

Taxpayer Identification Number (TIN) and Employer Identification Number (EIN)

Another requisite identification number for Healthcare Entrepreneurs is the Taxpayer Identification Number (TIN) provided by the IRS. Taxpayers often are confused about the difference between a TIN and its close cousin, the Employer Identification Number (EIN), which is sometimes referred to as an Employer Registration Number (ERN). The numbers are the same for each business entity. The difference lies in their purpose.

Whether or not you plan to have employees, you must apply for and receive a TIN. You can do this online at www.irs.gov/individuals/international-taxpayers/taxpayer-identification-numbers-tin. Your business will be assigned a nine-digit number to serve as both a TIN and an EIN. When you are paying taxes for the company, your company is referenced by the TIN; when you are recording your employees' taxes, the number is called an EIN. The EIN is used for other purposes as well, including opening a bank account.

Business Licenses

Some local governments require business licenses, sometimes called occupational licenses. If required, business licenses must be obtained from the county, the city, or from both, depending on the locale.

> **TIP:** If appropriate, obtain licenses and permits for specific functions such as biomedical waste disposal and drug storage.

Laws and codes governing these licenses can be confusing. Some jurisdictions require only one license per corporation; others require a separate license for each address used by a practice. Still others insist that every licensed professional practicing in the jurisdiction have their own individual business license even if the licensed professional is working for a corporation that already has a license in its name.

Certificates of Occupancy (CO)

Whether you are leasing existing space or building a new office from the ground up, many jurisdictions require at least one Certificate of Occupancy (CO). This is, as the name implies, the certificate that says you may occupy and use your office for your stated purpose(s). The CO most often can be obtained from the county government; however, in some areas, the municipality controls COs. In other jurisdictions, you may need to obtain a CO from both the county and the municipality.

CHECKLIST 1

Commonly Required Permits And Licenses

Permit/License Type	Apply To
Federal	
National Provider Identification Number (NPI)	National Plan and Provider Enumeration System (PECOS)
Provider Transaction Tracking Number (PTAN)	Centers for Medicare & Medicaid Services Contractors (MAC)
Taxpayer Identification Number/ Employer Identification Number (TIN/EIN)	U.S. Department of Revenue, Internal Revenue Service
Drug Enforcement Agency Number (DEA)	U.S. Drug Enforcement Agency
Clinical Laboratory License (CLIA)	Centers for Medicare & Medicaid Services
State	
Professional License	State professional board
Sales Tax License	State Department of Revenue
Pollution Control Permit	State, city, and/or county environmental protection agency
Local	
Certificate of Occupancy (CO)	City and/or county building department
Local Business License	City and/or county licensing department
Biomedical Waste Permit	State and/or local department of environmental health
Fire Department Permit	Local fire district
Sign Permit	City and/or county zoning department

Use this checklist to make sure you haven't missed any of the more commonly required permits and licenses. You may not be required to have some of these items, but it is wise to inquire in your locale.

Jurisdictions typically consider several factors when granting COs. Compliance with building and zoning codes is chief among these factors. Many locales have special requirements for medical professionals. For example, medical services might require more parking spaces than other businesses. In some jurisdictions, unique requirements for medical businesses are applied to all healthcare professionals whose profession is not explicitly listed elsewhere in the governing code. In other jurisdictions, professions that are not explicitly listed as medical are treated the same as any other non-healthcare business. It is essential to make sure that the space you are leasing, buying, or building is legally and physically suitable for your purposes. See Checklist 1 for a list of commonly required permits and licenses.

Starting Up Your Business

TIP: Even if you have been in practice for many years, it will be worth your while to read the portions of this book that address the opening of a new practice. Most practices open under circumstances that do not allow the owner or owners to build the infrastructure that is necessary for that practice to reach its full financial potentials. Therefore, even if you are an experienced businessperson, you can benefit from reading the following sections with an eye toward identifying and filling in the gaps in an existing practice.

We have all heard the expression "location, location, location." There is wisdom in this saying. The location of your practice will have a significant impact on your financial success.

FINDING AND MAKING A HOME FOR YOUR PRACTICE

As with all major business decisions, begin by clarifying your goals and objectives. These should be written into your business plan along with the information you discover about the various locations you consider. Although other factors may come into play, the location you choose should optimize your chances of achieving your goals and objectives over both the near term and the long term.

Research geographic areas in which patients who would be likely to use your services live. Epidemiologic data, available online, can help narrow the field by identifying places that have large populations of people who will need your services. Most states publish some epidemiologic data, including summary reports and reports of hospital traffic that include diagnoses. In military jargon, you are in search of a "target-rich environment."

Just because a region is "target-rich" does not necessarily mean it is a good choice, however. Other practitioners in your field also may have chosen to practice there because of the number of potential patients, so it is important to learn how many professionals are competing for the same patients. The ratio of potential patients to competitors is a statistic you can use to compare options.

Once you have homed in on a manageable number of office options, take a closer look at each. A good starting place is the U.S. Census Bureau, which can be accessed at www.census.gov. In addition to accessing neatly summarized tables of pre-packaged information, you can search for data using a variety of criteria and data points. Many real estate sites also offer key information about the vicinity surrounding a given address or neighborhood. For a fee, several companies will do this research for you using the publicly available databases or their own proprietary web crawler algorithms.

As you research potential office locations, consider several demographic factors, such as average household income, access to disposable income, and other indicators of ability to pay. Obviously, being within easy driving distance of one or more population centers is important. Although there certainly are some exceptions to the rule, patients usually search for services that are located near their residence. Ease of access is an oft-cited factor when patients are asked why they chose a particular professional.

The density of the population is a factor, but is a double-edged sword. Higher population density may mean more potential patients living nearby, but it also may mean difficulties getting to your office. The age of the population is important as well. It would make little sense for a Reproductive Endocrinologist to set up a practice in a neighborhood where the average age is in the late 40s.

At the bottom line, the savvy Healthcare Entrepreneur knows what demographics describe their most desirable patients and chooses office space that is convenient for people who fit those demographics.

Choosing Office Space: The Cost-to-Benefit Ratio

Although the location of a business is important, the cost of occupying the space (i.e., rent, mortgage payment, taxes, etc.) influences where you might choose to set up shop. Every budget has its limits, and costs must be considered. However, it is an error to consider the rent or mortgage payment amount as a single number. In fact, the costs of space are best understood as a ratio of cost-to-benefit.

The benefit part of the ratio could involve the number of additional patients you might have in a more convenient location, the visibility of the office on main traffic arteries, the proximity to referral sources, and the financial demographics of the surrounding region. For example, a group of Audiologists would be well-advised to consider paying higher rent for office space in a medical building that already houses a large ear, nose, and throat practice.

When looking at real estate, it is also important to consider the vitality of the neighborhood. This is a multifaceted process. Determine whether the surrounding area is growing or declining economically. Most local governments will provide business owners with information on the economic status of a block or neighborhood. Use this information to make sure you are not moving into a building that will lose its appeal. Savvy Healthcare Entrepreneurs are not tempted to search for space based solely on what is affordable at the moment.

As is the case when you consider a neighborhood for your home, it is important to learn about your neighbors before agreeing to lease or purchase space in a multitenant building. Your business neighbors may influence how often there are problems in the building and what sorts of customers come to the building.

Imagine, for example, a high-end cosmetic surgery practice located in a building in which another tenant offers Suboxone treatments for intravenous drug addicts and counseling for recently released convicts. Know thy neighbor and make sure the lease or condominium documents set appropriate restrictions and parameters.

Buy, Rent, or Lease

There are many ways to invest in your business, including purchasing, rather than leasing, the physical plant in which your business is located. On the one hand, owning a building increases the financial risks associated with your practice. Buying a building means putting more eggs in that one basket. On the other hand, owning your building helps diversify your investment portfolio and gives you more control over the likely value of the investment. That is not to say that buying gives you complete control. Consider whether land values are appreciating, stable, or depreciating.

Risk factors aside, owning your building brings increased responsibility and less flexibility should you decide to move; however, a well-chosen property may provide some financial advantages while you are building your investment portfolio.

Freestanding buildings are not the only option when it comes to buying office space; buying an office condominium is often another option. This option may be attractive due to relatively lower costs and the proximity to other healthcare professionals. It is *essential*, not just important, to read and understand the documents that govern a condominium (see Checklist 2). These include, but are not limited to, the bylaws, declarations, and rules. As is always the case with important and complex documents, it is worth having an Attorney read them so you know what you are getting into.

CHECKLIST 2

Documents To Check Before Purchasing a Condominium

1. Articles of incorporation
2. Bylaws
3. Rules and regulations
4. Budgets (past, current, and proposed)
5. Minutes of recent meetings

Finishing out an existing space or building from scratch may be the only way to have your office configured the way you want it. Having your space laid out the way you've envisioned can contribute to increased productivity. Keep in mind, however, that over time, the ideal configuration is likely to change. This can be due to endogenous factors, such as the growth of the practice, or exogenous factors, such as changes in technology that require different types of space. It is important, therefore, to think through the likely changes your business will experience as far out in time as you are able.

Building from square one can be much more expensive than other options, especially when you consider the value of your own time. Some of the planning and oversight can be delegated to architects, consultants, and even spouses, but you should be heavily involved at every step of the process. You are the only one who knows firsthand how your space will be used and how even minor changes can enhance or detract from its efficiency.

When building or buying a space, you likely will benefit financially from mortgaging the expense. Mortgages may have hidden costs, however. Lenders use closing costs, appraisal fees, and other expenses to boost profits on loans that are advertised at attractive interest rates. When borrowing money to purchase an office, consider these sometimes-hidden costs.

Leasing or Renting Office Space

In common parlance, the terms "leasing" and "renting" are often used interchangeably. In fact, despite many similarities, leasing differs from renting in that leasing connotes a longer-term commitment from both parties. Accordingly, some of the points of negotiation associated with leasing may not be necessary in a short-term renting circumstance.

> **TIP:** Talk to colleagues about what they wish was different in their office layout. Learn from their mistakes.

For many Healthcare Entrepreneurs, leasing space is a more attractive option than buying or building. There are, in fact, several advantages to leasing. For example, leasing tends to require less working capital than buying or building. In addition, leasing allows a bit more flexibility if and when you want to relocate your office.

On the other hand, if you don't own your space, someone else has significant influence over your practice. Consider, for example, the landlord who announces their intent not to renew your lease when it expires because they have a larger tenant who wants more space. In effect, the landlord would be compelling your practice to relocate.

Always have written agreements when accepting responsibility for office space or other real property.

Reviewing a Real Estate Lease

When it comes to leasing space, the rental amount may be complicated by the different variables that landlords manipulate in order to get their price. It is not uncommon for landlords to advertise a reasonably attractive rental rate and then, after a prospective tenant shows interest, announce that there is also a fee for Common Area Maintenance (CAM). CAM fees typically cover things such as the landlord's property taxes, the costs of selected utilities, landscaping, and other common area expenses associated with running a building. The CAM may be expressed as a fixed dollar amount, but more often is expressed as dollars per square foot of space rented.

The impact of CAM fees can be substantial. For example, if a tenant agrees to lease a 1000-square-foot space at $20 per square foot, they reasonably expect the rent expense to be $20,000 per year ($20 x 1,000) or $1,666.67 per month. If there is also a CAM fee of $5 per square foot, the actual cost of leasing the space is increased by 25% or $5,000 per year. The actual monthly cost is $2,083.33 ($25,000 per year).

In most locales, rental fees are subject to sales taxes, which must also be considered when budgeting. In addition to the $20,000 per year for rental costs in the example above, the sales tax would be $1,600 per year in a jurisdiction that levies an 8% sales tax. In this example, a space that seemed to cost $20,000 per year has ballooned to $26,600 per year. That is considerably higher than the original expectation and may make the space in question infeasible.

> **TIP:** Before committing to a space, check the quality and strength of the internet and cell phone signals in that space.

The cost of utilities must also be taken into account. Utilities include water, sewer, garbage collection, electricity, telephone services, and internet access. The costs usually will be the same or similar from building to building in the same county, city, or nearby town, but this is not always the case. For example, different buildings are wired for services from different Internet Service Providers (ISPs). When you are selecting a location for your business, you may also be narrowing your choices for ISPs. This can have implications for the cost and quality of your internet access. Naturally, lower-quality internet access can negatively affect your office's productivity. With so many practice management software programs stored in the internet cloud, unreliable internet service can be disruptive to your business.

Another element of the lease that deserves attention is who is financially responsible for the maintenance and repair of building systems. Ideally, the responsibility remains with the landlord, but many leases shift some, if not all, of that burden to the tenant. Heating and air-conditioning equipment repair and maintenance can be among the most expensive costs.

Consider the difference between a lease that requires the tenant to have and use an annual air-conditioning maintenance contract versus a lease that requires the tenant to have the same contract and be responsible for repairing the air-conditioning system if and when it breaks. In the latter case, if the equipment is irreparable, the tenant must buy the landlord a new heating and air-conditioning system.

Like all contracts, leases have what Attorneys refer to as "term and termination" language. This language addresses how long the lease will last and the conditions upon which it will terminate. In general, the longer the lease, the lower the monthly cost of leasing the property. Many landlords propose high lease rates and leave it to the prospective tenant to ask for and negotiate a lower rate. If you are willing to sign a longer-term lease, you should ask for lower rates than those charged for tenants who are on shorter-term leases. Savvy Healthcare Entrepreneurs actively and unabashedly negotiate the terms of every lease.

Most leases also have what is referred to as an "escalator clause." This clause prescribes an annual increase in rent throughout the term of the lease. Sometimes the increase is expressed simply as a flat percentage of the previous year's rent; other escalators are tied to economic indices, such as the cost-of-living index. Escalator clauses protect the landlord from the rising costs of running the building; however, the tenant faces increasingly higher rents.

It is always worthwhile to negotiate with the landlord to ensure the escalator clause is removed from the lease or, at a minimum, set at a reasonable rate. Although businesses in most industries can raise their rates to offset increases in the cost of living, healthcare fees are often fixed over time, so even a small increase in rent may constitute an actual loss at the bottom line of your business.

Offices for rent come in all sorts of configurations. Some spaces are configured as shells with no interior walls; others have been previously occupied and are configured with walls, plumbing, and electrical wiring in place. As you consider how best to configure your space, remember that if you are leasing, you likely will be responsible for restoring the space to its original condition when the lease ends. So, don't knock down walls or make other significant structural changes without the landlord's written consent and written assurance that the changes you make will be accepted as "original condition."

New tenants typically are offered build-out allowances if they will be occupying an office shell. Build-out allowances are the monies, or other considerations, a landlord provides to get a space configured to a tenant's liking. When the space under consideration is an empty shell, a build-out allowance should certainly be a part of the negotiations. Such allowances can often also be negotiated when an already-finished space needs an upgrade or alteration. Although not technically part of a build-out allowance, items like new carpet and fresh paint should be discussed even if the space is suitable for occupancy as is.

Remember, when you are renting, any and all improvements belong to the landlord. Consider soundproofing, for example. The landlord may have budgeted for standard wall construction and standard insulation in walls. You may want more insulation and sound-reducing wall construction between adjacent examination rooms to protect the confidentiality of patient-doctor conversations. The landlord may try to pass that extra expense to you, pointing out that subsequent tenants will be perfectly content with standard construction. Regardless, such points should be negotiated.

Few spaces are suitable for immediate occupancy without some modifications. The modifications can range from simple and easy to complex. One often overlooked pre-occupancy activity has to do with cleaning the office space. This includes cleaning the air-conditioning vents so that any accumulated mold and other toxins do not present a problem. Likewise, cleaning carpets and repainting walls should be addressed prior to moving in. Ideally, you can negotiate to shift those costs to the landlord.

Many landlords ask for "first and last month's rent" to be paid in advance of moving into an office. From the landlord's perspective, the last month's rent can be used if the tenant fails to pay the rent at the end of the lease term. The landlord can use another portion of the sum, the security deposit, to repair damages after a tenant moves out. Unless otherwise prescribed by law, leases should be negotiated to specify that monies paid in advance be held in interest-bearing accounts and that the resulting interest belongs to you, the tenant.

Laws governing how security deposits can be used vary from jurisdiction to jurisdiction. Regardless, it is worth negotiating with the landlord to ensure that the lease clearly states how the security deposit can be used and under what conditions it must be returned in full. To avoid possible disagreements about the condition of the space before and after occupancy, make a video of the entire space before moving in and ensure any change to the property, including relatively minor things such as hanging diplomas, are approved in writing by the landlord.

Deposits and other advance payments should appear on your company's balance sheets so your company is credited for that asset. This, along with a note on your calendar, also reminds you to ask for the money deposited when you leave the leased space.

Property Insurance for Leased Space

If you lease your office space, the landlord may insist that you pay for property insurance. This expense, which can be substantial, may tilt the equation in terms of how affordable a given space is. It may be possible to negotiate with the landlord to reduce or remove the requirement for property insurance; however, it is understandable when a landlord refuses to do so. In that case, make sure the requirements of the lease are reasonable.

All too often, leases require coverages at high levels such as $1 million per occurrence and $2 million in aggregate for a property that is not worth $1 million on the open market. Negotiating the coverage limits to a more reasonable level makes this expense more tolerable.

The names used to describe different types of leases can be confusing. Although there are subsets to each class of lease, most leases fall into one of four categories (see Table 2). Gross leases require the tenant to pay a predictable fixed amount of rent each month. Expenses such as property tax, maintenance, and insurance are built into the fixed rent amount. With a Gross lease, the landlord is at risk if any of the costs of running the building increase.

Net leases call for the tenant to pay a fixed rental price plus some combination of other costs which may fluctuate. In practical terms, the tenant shares some, or all of the risk from rising costs with the landlord. With a Triple Net lease the tenant agrees to accept all of the risk associated with paying for property taxes, insurance, maintenance and repairs. Double Net leases leave the responsibility for repairs and maintenance with the landlord while the tenant accepts responsibility for the property tax and insurance expenses. Although less commonly used, Single Net leases oblige the tenant to pay some or all of the property taxes. The savvy Healthcare Entrepreneur negotiates leases with an eye on the risk to reward ratios. The more risk the tenant must take, the lower the rent should be.

TABLE 2. Who Pays What in Different Types of Leases

Types of Leases	Gross Who Pays?		Single Net Who Pays?		Double Net Who Pays?		Triple Net Who Pays?	
	Tenant	Landlord	Tenant	Landlord	Tenant	Landlord	Tenant	Landlord
Rent	X		X		X		X	
Sales Tax	X		X		X		X	
Property Tax		X	X		X		X	
Insurance		X		X	X		X	
Maintenance		X		X		X	X	

What About Parking?

Adequate parking is important for the success of any business. Local ordinances often dictate a minimum number of parking spaces that each building must have, depending on the types of businesses housed in the building. Often, medical offices require more parking spaces per square foot of interior office space than other types of offices.

Even buildings that have legally sufficient parking may not meet your needs. Factors such as reserved spaces for preferred tenants and neighboring tenants running high-traffic businesses can leave your patients driving around the parking lot in frustration and arriving late for appointments.

The Importance of Signage

Signage is another factor to consider before leasing, buying, or building an office space. Well-placed, effective signs serve as marketing tools that can promote your business and guide people to your office. Large signs that are prominently placed and visible from the street serve both the marketing and the guidance functions. Signs buried in a raft of other signs are of little value.

Signs in parking areas or the lobby of your building are critical because they help new patients find your office and therefore affect patient flow. When your signs are inadequate in number, placement, information, or readability, patients may become confused. Patients who get lost due to poor signage may arrive late and in a frustrated state. Of course, this can wreak havoc with the scheduling flow dynamics of your office as well as the tenor of your relationship with a patient.

Rules about signage are usually controlled by local laws, the terms of a lease, or the bylaws of a condominium. Many jurisdictions limit the size and number of signs visible from a road and specify where signs can be placed in relation to a road. So, for example, if you are considering a building that houses several tenants, it is important to find out how much legally permissible outside signage space you will be allowed and where your sign will be placed. Your patients will not be able to readily pick out your sign if it has three-inch lettering and is in a field of 20 placards.

The same goes for interior signage. This ranges from listings in lobby directories to placards on or alongside your main entry. You should know in advance what is allowed and make sure the allowance will meet your needs and those of your patients. The deed, lease, or rental agreement should specify, in detail, the agreed-upon terms for signage.

EQUIPPING YOUR OFFICE

Selecting Furniture, Fixtures, and Equipment (FF&E) for your practice involves planning and research. The quality of the FF&E you buy will influence your professional image and dictate your need to repair or replace those items later. Consider your future equipment needs, including where large items will fit into your office. With technology improving at a rapid pace, it is also important to know whether the equipment you are considering is on the cutting edge or likely to be outdated in short order. The markup by FF&E sellers can be steep. Time invested in doing research, shopping around, and negotiating with sellers can pay you back in substantial savings.

> **TIP:** When budgeting for and ordering FF&E, don't forget to take into account the costs of sales taxes, shipping, handling, and set-up.

Keep tax considerations in mind when purchasing FF&E. Capital equipment can be depreciated on your income taxes over time. In most years, the depreciation will reduce your tax burden. In practical terms, your actual cost for these items is partially reduced by the offset. On the other hand, most capital items lose value over time.

Inventory and track these items as capital assets on your business's balance sheet. Doing so makes it easier for your Accountant (and, therefore, cheaper for you) to file your corporate taxes. In addition, many jurisdictions have what is sometimes referred to as a Tangible Assets Tax (TAT), which is a tax on the value of your business at the end of a tax period. The value of the business's possessions is part of the overall value of the business. By keeping track of your FF&E and the associated depreciation, you can accurately pay your tangible assets taxes.

Lease or Buy?

Capital items often can be leased rather than purchased. The considerations regarding which route to take are quite like those surrounding the decision to lease or purchase office space. There are, however, some differences. One particularly important difference involves the usable lifespan of equipment. Although it is possible to give an outdated office a facelift, outdated equipment should be replaced. Leasing provides a bit more flexibility when it comes time to update your equipment.

Computers, copiers, and other electronics are examples of equipment with a short usable life expectancy. A benefit of purchasing equipment such as computers is that the equipment can be depreciated in your tax accounting over a short time frame. However, considering that the usable life of today's computers is roughly equal to, or less than, the time frame for depreciation, if you want to capture the maximum advantage of depreciation, you must replace the equipment every few years.

When it comes time to do so, the resale value of the old computers can be negligible. Leasing, on the other hand, allows the business owner to keep monthly costs down while providing the flexibility to keep up with changing technology. Often, leased equipment comes with free repair and maintenance.

> **TIP:** The costs and losses associated with computer and telephone failures can be substantial. It may be more cost-effective to pay a bit extra to have a repair business "on-call" with a guaranteed rapid response time.

Consider equipment maintenance and repair prior to purchase. When equipment breaks down in the middle of a busy day at a busy practice, the impact can be profound — that's not the time to start searching for repair services. As a general rule, the extended warranties offered with electronics are more costly than other options and should be eschewed. When possible, establish and maintain a relationship with a reputable electronic equipment repair vendor who is familiar with your equipment and whose fees are known in advance. The same principle applies to mechanical equipment such as heating and air-conditioning equipment.

Considering Telephone Systems

Telephone systems are your business's link to the outside world. There are several types of telephone systems to consider, ranging from simple single-line phones to complex multiline computer-based systems.

A very small business might buy a number of one-, two-, or three-line handsets at a local business supply store; however, all but the smallest of businesses will want or need more features than this option typically brings. Most Healthcare Entrepreneurs will require a more sophisticated telephone system.

Choosing the right system for your business begins with your business plan. From the business plan, you can determine how many employees you anticipate will need phones in the coming years, how many locations must be served, and how many Receptionists you will need to handle incoming calls. These variables help guide you to the right-sized system.

Next, determine which features you need and which you want but can live without. Some features, such as call parking, may be essential; others, such as videoconferencing, may be a nice luxury but may be used so infrequently that they qualify as an unnecessary expense. Still others, such as having a text message transcribing all voice mails sent to your mobile phone, may prove to be an impediment to your efficiency.

Telephone systems are often packaged to entice buyers to purchase a higher tier of products and services than the buyer needs. Features may be bundled together, and desirable features may be included only in the costlier bundles. Remember, the more features you purchase, the higher the possibility of a breakdown.

The practice's main telephone number, the number shown on business cards and in advertisements, should be set to roll over. Rolling over means that calls made to the main number will be directed to another line or lines when the main line is in use. Rollovers should be limited to the number of lines your Receptionists can handle.

> **TIP:** Many practices add one or more back-lines on which emergency calls from employees and family members can be received. The back-line telephone number should be shared with a limited number of people.

Some personnel, such as Collections Specialists, need ready access to an outgoing telephone line. Likewise, Clinical personnel often need to be able to return messages between patients. So, it is a good idea to have one or more telephone lines that are reserved for outgoing calls only. The number of additional lines for outgoing calls should be determined by the pattern and volume of outgoing calls in your practice. It is rare that everyone in a group needs to be on the phone at once. Train everyone in your office to avoid using incoming lines for outgoing calls.

Voice-Over-Internet Protocol (VOIP) technology has become increasingly popular. These are systems that use the internet instead of old-fashioned telephone lines. Early problems with call clarity have been fixed to some degree but are not yet wholly addressed. These systems tend to be fully featured, easily scaled, readily able to serve multiple offices, and once installed, relatively inexpensive to maintain.

COMPUTER SOFTWARE AND WEBSITE RESOURCES

Computers, computer software, and internet websites have become integral parts of the infrastructure in every industry, including healthcare. Properly chosen software and the thoughtful use of appropriate websites allow businesses, and the personnel who run those businesses, to function efficiently. Healthcare Entrepreneurs stay ahead of the curve by making use of these resources and incorporating new software and internet resources as they become available.

Software for Billing

Purchasing billing software is similar to buying a car, at least insofar as both purchases tend to involve a basic model onto which you can add several optional features. At its most basic, a billing program keeps track of charges accrued, fees due, and payments made for services rendered. For some small boutique practices in which fees are almost always paid at the time of service, this basic program can be quite enough to meet the needs of the practice.

The more heavily involved a practice becomes in insurance billing, billing for multiple professionals, and managing Accounts Receivable, the more valuable the optional features become. At a minimum, features such as accurate and understandable reporting are essential. A program that skimps on its reporting functions deprives the Healthcare Entrepreneur of information that can and should be used to make important business decisions.

Consider, for example, the value of a report that tells you how much of your usual fee was written off as an insurance contract discount or bad debt versus the same report broken down by referral sources. The latter report may reveal valuable points of business intelligence, such as the fact that a colleague who frequently refers patients to you is consistently sending patients who contribute little to the profitability of your practice.

Consider the value of the referral analysis report shown in Table 3. At a glance, the Healthcare Entrepreneur can obtain vital information that guides marketing and public relations efforts. In this report, negative numbers are surrounded by brackets.

Noting the decline in referrals from Drs. Freud and Mayo, the savvy Healthcare Entrepreneur would call both of them to reestablish the relationship and ensure there are no problems underlying the decline in referrals shown in the second column. The Healthcare Entrepreneur also may reconsider the value of referrals from Dr. Mayo, whose patients, at least during the dates under consideration, seem to pay poorly. Perhaps Dr. Mayo can be persuaded to reevaluate his referral patterns to ensure a more heterogeneous referral mix, or it may be necessary to politely decline referrals from Dr. Mayo.

TABLE 3. Referral Analysis

Referral Source	Patients	Number of New	Visits	Charges	Payments	Write-Off	Written Off	Visit
Apgar, Virginia	5	4	16	$2,480.00	$1,343.63	$1,136.37	46%	$83.98
Barnard, Christiaan	0	(6)	0	$0.00	$0.00	$0.00		
Freud, Sigmund	12	0	15	$2,325.00	$1,860.00	$465.00	20%	$124.00
Mayo, Charles	6	2	6	$930.00	$0.00	$930.00	100%	$0.00

Most billing programs allow you to electronically transmit bills to patients and third-party payers. A range of technological sophistication goes along with this feature. Basic programs simply transmit the data that you or a staff member have entered. Missing or inaccurate information goes undetected and the claim may, therefore, be rejected by the clearinghouse that processes the claim. These rejections can be quite costly in terms of both cash flow and the time needed to correct and retransmit the claim.

At the other end of the spectrum are programs that evaluate each claim in a process known as "scrubbing." These programs alert you to problems with a claim before the claim is submitted to a payer. These programs allow you to consistently generate "clean claims" that are more likely to be paid the first time they are submitted.

Entering payment data into a billing program can be time-consuming and, therefore, expensive. Healthcare is one of the few industries in which payments often are made in dribs and drabs, thus increasing the cost of bookkeeping.

Consider, for example, a simple $180 office procedure rendered early in the calendar year to a patient who has traditional Medicare coverage and a secondary insurance policy. If the patient still has an amount due on the Medicare deductible, this amount must be collected and recorded. When Medicare pays its portion of the bill, that payment must also be entered into the billing program. At the same time, the bill must be adjusted to account for the difference between the amount billed and the amount Medicare allows for that service. Then, when the secondary insurer pays its share, yet another entry must be made into the billing program. The costs of data entry add up and can be considerable.

To spare some of these costs, some billing programs automatically apply amounts shown in Electronic Remittance Advisories (ERAs) to the appropriate account. This feature is not always available in the less-expensive, bare-bones billing software programs, so it is often overlooked by buyers who are trying to keep the cost of such software to a minimum. However, for many practices, the cost of manually entering each and every charge and payment exceeds the costs of paying for a more expensive program that does that work for you. The prudent Healthcare Entrepreneur weighs the costs of more sophisticated billing programs against the cost of paying people to manually enter the data and the cost of slower cash flow.

> **TIP:** There are expenses associated with everything you do on a patient's behalf. When patients do not pay, these expenses become a loss.

Software for Scheduling Appointments

An ever-dwindling number of professionals still keep track of their schedules using paper-and-pencil calendars and appointment books. Most of today's Healthcare Entrepreneurs rely on electronic appointment-tracking software. The efficiency of electronic scheduling primarily comes from three sources: (1) the ability to search for an open appointment time or an existing appointment; (2) access to a secure portal through which patients can make, confirm, and change their own appointments, thus saving staff time; and (3) the complete integration of the scheduling program into an overall practice management system. These programs are fully integrated into, or at least mesh with, billing and other practice management functions, thus saving time and reducing errors such as missed billings.

It is helpful when choosing scheduling software to use some criteria that salespeople seldom mention. For example, how many screens must a user go through to accomplish a routine function such as changing an appointment? How often must you switch from mouse to keyboard? How far must you move the mouse to go through the required steps? Although streamlined design engineering does not necessarily mean that the underlying software is superior in all ways, the fact that the software engineers invested time and effort in addressing human factors bodes well for the ease of using the system, which saves staff time and money.

Electronic Health Records

Under pressure from the government and other entities, much of the healthcare community has converted from paper records to Electronic Health Records (EHRs). These are the digital versions of the old-fashioned paper charts in which healthcare professionals tracked their notes and other information about the health of each patient.

As with most software, your investment in the EHR system is likely to be substantial. The costs are not limited to purchasing, leasing, and usage fees. Installation can be quite time-consuming, even when the vendor facilitates the initial migration of data from your previous system. Staff training and the time spent addressing errors made during training are among the costs to take into account (see Table 4).

TABLE 4. Questions To Ask When Selecting An EHR Program

> EHR programs are similar to robots in that they perform tasks for the user. Some tasks occur automatically in response to pre-programmed criteria; others require a user command. The more sophisticated the EHR, the more costly it can be, so choose those features that save enough time and money to offset the costs of the relevant function.
>
> ♦ How does the program comply with the HIPAA privacy and security standards?
> ♦ In what ways doesn't the program integrate with the associated practice management software?
> ♦ What are the recurring costs that come with this software and how often can they be increased?
> ♦ Which dictation software can be used to dictate notes and reports?
> ♦ What information can be set to automatically populate across fields?
> ♦ Can more than one user access a patient's records at the same time?
> ♦ What reports are available to help make use of the data in the EHR?
> ♦ What information will the vendor load for you and what information must the buyer enter?
> ♦ In what formats does the program accept documents generated elsewhere?
> ♦ Are alerts available when patients have similar names?
> ♦ What databases are embedded in the program and how can they be searched?
> ♦ Can the program be set to follow each user's unique workflow?
> ♦ How well does the program articulate with the laboratories, pharmacies, and other entities to which you send orders and from which you receive reports?
> ♦ Does the program notify the user when reports of diagnostic studies arrive electronically?
> ♦ Does the program flag charts when a consent, authorization, or signature is missing?
> ♦ Does the program crosscheck patient allergies and medications when new prescriptions are entered?

Treat your decision to invest in EHRs as you would any investment: Do your homework. This includes calculating the Return On Investment (ROI). In other words, ask yourself how this purchase will help generate profits or, at least, pay for itself. If, as is often the case with EHRs, the investment cannot be turned into a profit, search for other expense items that can be cut to rebalance the budget.

Although the terms are used interchangeably in day-to-day practice, Electronic Medical Records (EMRs) are not technically the same as EHRs. EMRs are the electronic records you keep in your office or facility for each patient; EHRs are the digital locations for each patient's entire healthcare record. Hospital records, for example, include information from the attending physician, consultants, nurses, and any number of other professionals.

> **TIP:** Patients move their residences and insurance coverage changes. It is a good idea to re-confirm the accuracy of the contact and insurance information for each patient at every visit.

Nearly all EHRs allow for the electronic Health Information Exchange (HIE). HIE allows the EHR to transfer information from and to other EMRs. Most of the time this occurs when a Healthcare Entrepreneur intentionally sends information in a process known as Direct Exchange. With appropriate authorizations clinicians can also locate and/or request information using Query-Based Exchange protocols. Although not technically HIE, some EHR and EMR programs are sophisticated enough that electronic biometric monitoring data can also be fed directly into and stored in the program.

Most EHR programs offer portals through which patients can gain direct access to their records. Nearly all portals allow the patient to input basic demographic information, contact information, and insurance identification numbers, which saves staff time. More sophisticated portals also allow patients to enter other pertinent data, such as contact information for their next of kin or healthcare surrogate, and their health history. Known collectively as Personal Health Records (PHRs), these records engage patients as contributing members of their own healthcare record-keeping team.

Insurance Confirmation Websites

Once a patient's information has been entered into your system, it often is necessary to confirm the patient's insurance coverage. This can be accomplished in any of several ways. One way to verify insurance coverage is to call the insurance company at the number printed on the back of most insurance cards. Doing so is notoriously time-consuming, as a great deal of time is often spent on hold while the caller waits to talk with an insurance company representative, who is invariably delayed "due to unusually heavy call volume."

An alternative is to enter the patient's information into any of several websites that report the specific terms, allowances, and limitations of an insurance policy. These sites include those that belong to the particular insurance company and some, such as Availity, that provide information on behalf of several carriers. Although there is typically a cost for the service, some of the more sophisticated billing programs will contact the insurer for you with the push of a button. Not only does this save money by reducing the demand on staff time, it also can save money by warning your office when a patient's insurance policy has lapsed or entered a new deductible phase.

> **TIP:** Information provided by insurance companies is not always up to date. Make sure that your contracts with patients and payers allow you to be paid when a claim is denied even though you provided services based on good faith reliance on information provided by the insurance carrier.

Accounting and Payroll Software

As a Healthcare Entrepreneur, you should consider investing in an accounting program such as QuickBooks or Peachtree. Even if you decide to outsource payroll and other accounting functions, these programs provide a reliable means of tracking the value of your practice, the costs of running it, and the information needed to pay taxes accurately. Although such programs take some time to master, they ensure that the information provided to Accountants and others is accurate and organized in a manner that leads to productive business decisions.

> **TIP:** YouTube provides training in most, and possibly all, of the programs you and your staff will use. Completing these trainings can bring to light helpful features that you otherwise might not use.

Many accounting programs offer payroll functions ranging in sophistication from merely allowing the user to enter and print payroll checks to filing federal, state, and local payroll taxes. Because payroll services and Accountants tend to be expensive, performing payroll functions in-house is often cost-effective.

> **TIP:** Federal regulations, known as the "red flag rules," require most healthcare professionals to confirm the identities of new patients by checking driver's licenses and other forms of identification, and by having an identity theft detection program in place. While some professionals are exempt, most are not.

Card Scanner Software

Copies of both sides of each new patient's driver's license and insurance card(s) should be part of your practice's intake paperwork. The driver's license, or other proof of identity, helps comply with federal red flag rules and can be helpful in collecting past-due fees. The copies of insurance cards come in handy when data is mis-transcribed or skipped when intake forms are being compiled. See Table 5 for key information you may need from patients' insurance cards.

Photocopying these documents is costly. Card scanners attached to each work station at which a patient might check in quickly pay for themselves with savings in both time and supplies.

Credit Card Payment Processors

Although it is possible to run a healthcare practice that does not accept credit cards, doing so risks alienating potential patients and reducing the rate of collections at your reception window. As a result, most Healthcare Entrepreneurs identify and

TABLE 5. Key Information From Insurance Cards

- The insured person's name and date of birth. (The patient may not be the insurance policy holder.)
- The Member ID number.
- The Group Name and/or Group Number.
- The plan type (i.e., PPO, HMO, etc.).
- Copayment amounts.
- Phone numbers to confirm benefits and obtain pre-authorizations.
- The address to which claims should be billed.

retain a credit card company through which payments can be processed. Vendors of credit card services are frequently referred to as "merchant services."

The realm of merchant services is filled with confusing terms, fees, rules, and surprising exceptions to rules, so the vendor selection process should be thought through carefully and reconsidered annually. Your bank can usually recommend vendors to you; however, it is a mistake to assume that a bank's recommendation means that the vendor will give you favorable rates and terms. Sometimes, the opposite is true. See Table 6 for an overview of common merchant services fees.

TABLE 6. Merchant Services Summary

	# of Items	Transaction	Fee Category	Fees
Sales	350	$105,000.29	Visa/MC/Disc	$5,223.58
Returns	1	$150.00	AmEx	$1,042.16
Net Sales	351	$104,850.29	Debit	–
Chargebacks	3	$927.00	Chargeback Fees	$27.81
TOTAL SALES	**354**	**$103,923.29**	Authorization Fees	$15.77
			Association Fees	$89.67
			Monthly Fee	$20.00
			Other Fees	$72.13
			TOTAL FEES	**$6,491.12**

Credit card companies are like insurance companies in that they are in the business of finance. That is, most of their earnings come from investing the money they receive from others, not from the fees they charge you. Although, at least in theory, the financial sector is heavily regulated, you need go no further than the economic crisis of the early 21st century to appreciate that the protection offered by such regulations is questionable.

Credit card salespeople often cite their "qualifying rate" when they explain how their program operates. The qualifying rate is their most favorable rate; however, it typically is reserved for high-volume customers and often comes with a number of restrictions. A Healthcare Entrepreneur may be able to negotiate the best possible rate even when, technically, they do not qualify for that rate. Any time you do agree to a higher rate, you should obtain new bids a year or so later. An annual review of credit card usage and costs provides the information needed to either renegotiate fees with your current vendor or choose a new vendor.

The primary fee credit card companies charge Healthcare Entrepreneurs is the percentage of each sale that the credit card company keeps for themselves. This is known as the "discounting rate." Regardless of what the primary discounting rate is, most contracts call for a higher fee when other types of credit cards are used or other data entry criteria are not met. For example, when a credit card offers the card holder airline miles or cash back, the discounting rate is likely to be higher than the basic rate. In essence, the merchant (i.e., you) ends up helping fund the patient's next first-class airline seat upgrade. Likewise, if a credit card is manually entered, as is often the case when payments are made over the telephone, you are likely to pay a higher fee.

In addition to the various discounting rates, most credit card services charge an array of other fees. Some vendors even charge for customer service calls when the vendor's service is out of commission.

Fees for routine services such as accessing your merchant services account online are also popular in this industry. Even when a patient's charge dispute is deemed baseless, you may be charged a fee for having the dispute handled. There can even be fees for mandatory actions that serve the credit card company's interests, such as a call to report a stolen credit card. Fees for terminating your relationship with a merchant services vendor are endemic in this industry and inhibit Healthcare Entrepreneurs who may be considering changing to another vendor.

The prudent Healthcare Entrepreneur negotiates each and every fee with the credit card salesperson. Once the salesperson says the offer cannot be sweetened any further, it is worth using your previous experience with credit cards to estimate the actual costs of the terms you are considering accepting before you sign the contract. By dividing the amount of money that was charged through your account by the total fees you are charged, you can calculate your "effective rate," which is the actual cost, expressed as a percent, of doing business with that vendor.

Another cost of accepting credit cards involves the lag time between when your patient makes the payment and when that payment arrives in your bank account. Although money moves instantly across wireless networks, some credit card transactions still take days to complete. Just as insurance companies have an incentive to delay payments to professionals, credit card companies have an incentive to delay their outflows. Both use the money they are sitting on to profit from investments. Your contract should specify how long it will take for you to receive each payment. Ideally, the contract includes compensation to you when the actual lag time exceeds the lag time specified in the contract.

Accepting credit cards can involve expensive up-front costs, including setup, equipment, and software. A variety of terminals are available and range in price depending on their functionality. Regardless of whether you choose to lease or purchase a terminal, you may be asked to pay a separate fee for installation or software. These fees are often negotiable. Be wary of remarkably inexpensive machines. The attractive price might be related to a genuine sales incentive offer, but it may also mean that the machine is becoming out of date and will have to be replaced the next time the vendor upgrades its system.

Although most credit card terminals transmit information via the internet, some still operate through telephone lines. Of course, this requires an additional telephone line for this function. This cost sometimes can be mediated by setting up the credit card line so that it shares a line with a fax machine. This frugal approach can result in a "traffic jam" in your lobby as patients and staff alike wait for the shared line to be free so a credit card transaction can be completed.

The proliferation of tablets and smartphones has brought yet another option by which a business can process credit cards. Internet sites such as Square and its competitors allow Healthcare Entrepreneurs to swipe or enter credit card transactions directly into a smartphone or tablet. The rates for this service can be comparable and sometimes favorable when compared with the rates offered by traditional vendors. The portability is particularly attractive to Healthcare Entrepreneurs in small practices and those who offer services at remote locations.

Healthcare Entrepreneurs must be sure their vendor allows them to use these services without violating HIPAA and other laws governing patient confidentiality. It is a good idea to have patients who want to pay by credit card sign a form explicitly authorizing you to post charges to their card and acknowledging any potential risks associated with confidentiality.

Email Programs

Email has become an indispensable business tool in all industries. Whereas many companies can easily turn to off-the-shelf email readers such as Microsoft's Outlook or the email services that commonly come with web-hosting packages, healthcare professionals must take extra steps to ensure that emails are secure and compliant with laws governing privacy and confidentiality. Though costly and time-consuming to use, encryption programs are available with most email packages. Many EHR and EMR programs provide built-in encrypted email and messaging options.

It is wise to consider how accessible you want patient emails to be to you. Some professionals want patients to be able to reach them by email; others avoid emails from patients by keeping email addresses private and including warnings about the misuse of emails to ward off the liability that may come from a question asked by a patient in the form of an email.

There are pros and cons to each model. Certainly, making it easy for patients to communicate with their Healthcare Entrepreneur helps with patient engagement, patient loyalty, and patient retention. However, there are risks and expenses against which these gains must be weighed. Healthcare Entrepreneurs who accept emails or texts from patients must clearly advise their patients about the limits of this mode of communication and the potential for breaches of privacy. They must also have systems in place to ensure that emails are read and replied to in a timely, accurate manner.

Instant Messaging and Text Messaging

Instant Messaging (IM) and text messaging have become important options for communication. Bearing in mind the caveats regarding confidentiality discussed above, both options allow professionals and their staff members to communicate quickly about things that require immediate attention.

For example, without using the patient's name, a staff member may use IM or texting to advise a professional that a patient refused to pay a past-due balance when they checked in. In this way, a staff member does not need to physically track down the professional to pass on the information, and the professional can easily address the concerns with the patient.

Telehealth Programs

The COVID-19 pandemic spurred the use of telehealth into high gear as an accepted model of healthcare service delivery. Some practices invest in videoconferencing equipment and software; others rely on commercially available video conferencing websites. Some unique considerations should be borne in mind when it comes to purchasing or leasing such programs. Confidentiality is arguably chief among those considerations. Although it is tempting to use one of the available freeware videoconferencing programs, it is essential to choose a provider that allows for HIPPA-compliant encryption and privacy protection.

> **TIP:** When billing for telehealth services, be sure you are complying with the insurer's unique billing requirements. Some insurers require that the place of service code denote telehealth (code = 2) while others consider the location from which services were rendered to be the place of service. Some insurers want a

modifier code associated with the CPT codes billed when services were rendered via telehealth.

Before implementing a videoconferencing or telehealth session, make sure you obtain all the appropriate consents and follow required procedures. For example, patients you see via telehealth should still receive your Notice of Privacy Practices. Patients should be made aware of risks that are inherent in electronic communications such as hacking. Your consents should specifically address the implications of using telehealth. Also, make sure that your policies, procedures, and notices address how the digital footprint of these encounters will be stored and eventually destroyed.

Contact-Tracking Software

Healthcare Entrepreneurs encounter and conduct business with a wide range of people for a wide range of reasons. Everyone you encounter can be regarded as a member of your professional network. It is important to keep track of everyone's name and contact information. It is also helpful to keep track of other information such as the contracts and commitments you have with each of your contacts.

Contact tracking software is available to help organize this information. For example, billing software may serve as the contact tracker for patients, insurance companies, and payment guarantors; EHR software may keep track of referral sources; and a business-oriented program such as Outlook may track vendors, marketing targets, and other business contacts. Tracking all these functions in one program promotes significant efficiency. For most healthcare practices, the benefits of having a single source are outweighed by the costs.

Productivity-Enhancing Software

When examined closely, nearly everything you and your staff do involves numerous steps. Even basic tasks such as processing new patient registration forms constitute expense items that diminish profits. Computers often can perform routine tasks with more efficiency and less cost than their human counterparts. It can be an eye-opening and worthwhile exercise to think through routine office tasks in microscopic detail. Almost invariably, you will identify inefficiencies to address. Sometimes you will find that a task requires so much time, effort, or expense that it is financially more advantageous to automate that task.

Consider a routine self-referral from a prospective new patient. Before the electronics era, if that person called your office and got a busy signal, the prospect would have to hang up and call again later. Voicemail programs now capture the call, make a note of important information such as the caller's name and phone number, and, in many cases, send you an email or text advising you of the call, along with a written transcript of the voicemail message the caller left. The same program may have a feature that provides callers with information such as directions to your office. Such a program saves everyone time and thus improves productivity and profits.

Once contact has been made with the caller, an array of information must be obtained. Recording the minimum amount of data needed to establish a new patient can take 10 or more minutes of dialogue on the phone. Fortunately, programs now allow prospective patients to complete their own intake paperwork and transmit it electronically to your office staff. In some circumstances, the transmitted data must be entered manually; more sophisticated programs allow your computer to automatically populate data fields in your practice management program directly from the patient's entries.

Basic Office Software

Patients and professionals often bemoan the amount of paperwork that is required or seen as necessary in the healthcare industry. Forms ranging from clinical histories to laboratory results to required legal forms such as consents and authorizations must be prepared, printed, completed, and stored. Some practices handle these functions on paper, which is the most expensive approach. Costs include everything from buying paper to paying staff to handle the files. Increasingly, practices are turning to electronic means to complete these functions. Form-generating software, electronic signature pads, patient registration kiosks, and electronic scanners allow patients to complete forms more efficiently and at less cost of time and money to you.

Miscellaneous Office Software

Even practices that have invested in high-end EHR programs occasionally need word-processing programs to generate letters and other nonclinical documents. Likewise, many tech-savvy practices still need spreadsheet programs to help with budgeting and data analyses. PowerPoint and other presentation programs can be invaluable as marketing and training tools. Databases are helpful in practices that engage in functions that are best tracked separately from the clinical data.

Although such programs are being used less often in healthcare, many practices continue to buy the old standby suites of business programs such as Microsoft Office Suite for PCs and iWorks for Apple products. These are fine products loaded with helpful features, but such name-brand products can be costly to purchase, can require expensive updates, and in some cases, require a licensing fee. As more and more of the functions provided by these programs are transferred to industry-specific programs such as the EMR program, it is harder to justify these costs. Instead, freeware systems such as Open Office for PCs and LibreOffice for Apple products deserve consideration.

Data Storage and Destruction

Gone are the days of the ubiquitous banker's boxes into which paper records were placed for eternal storage or eventual destruction. Today, there are numerous options for document and data storage. Failure to plan for this critical business function can lead to costly inefficiencies and, at worst, steep fines. Unless your staff, including professional staff, are well trained in a uniform filing scheme, they will file documents, electronically or on paper, in whatever manner occurs to them at the moment. If and when that document must be retrieved, the costs of retrieval can skyrocket as expensive staff time is spent on a random hunt for the needed information. HIPAA and other consumer rights laws levy substantial fines when a requested record or portion of a requested record cannot be produced.

Laws governing how and how long records must be kept vary from jurisdiction to jurisdiction. Some state laws call for a longer period of retention than HIPAA does. Likewise, some managed care contracts require particularly lengthy records retention periods. So, it is essential that Healthcare Entrepreneurs not rely solely on HIPAA to guide their records management policies and procedures.

The use of Electronic Health Records is more common, but paper records are by no means dead. Many practices maintain correspondence, signed contracts, and other business documents, as well as a significant portion of medical records, on paper. Like their electronic counterparts, these documents should be stored using a system that ensures easy retrieval. This means that rules and conventions for filing are followed by all and that the data or documents are protected from loss. Important documents should always be scanned into electronic form even if the paper copy is retained.

One electronic storage option is a local server. This is essentially a computer owned and maintained by your business onto which files from all of your peripheral computers are directed. Files containing documents and other data can be stored on the server such that any authorized user can find what they need. Because more than one person can use the program, staff members can refer to each other's notes and can interchangeably help patients.

TIP: When your office's internet service goes down, you may be able to maintain internet access by creating a "hotspot" using your cellular telephone.

Servers should be backed up frequently with the backup copy stored in a remote location such as another server or in the cloud. Anyone who has attempted to do business with a company whose "server is down at the moment" knows how important servers are. When the server is not working, most, if not all, functions come to a grinding halt.

Cloud storage is similar to using a local computer server that is owned by the business, but the information is sent to geographically remote computer servers where the information is maintained in digital form. Cloud storage brings all the advantages of a server-based system plus some added benefits and some unique drawbacks.

Among the advantages is the fact that most cloud storage providers use redundant systems to make sure that the data are always backed up and available to users. Cloud storage is most efficient when the internet speed is good. Problems emerge when your business's internet service is interrupted, as cloud storage is reliant on access to the internet. When internet service goes down, the business may be shut down or, at least, hobbled until the service is restored. This can slow the access to many kinds of data, from clinical information to appointment schedules to billing and collections records.

Selecting servers and cloud storage providers can be a mind-bending, befuddling conundrum. Each vendor touts different benefits and features; few point out weaknesses and limitations. Not all cloud providers are HIPAA compliant, and some will not sign a HIPAA Business Associates Agreement.

Hidden costs can also be a problem. Although you can switch from one system or vendor to another if needed, such changes are costly in time and money. So, it is important to think carefully about your business' needs and make sure the system you select can and will consistently meet those needs. Once you have made your choice, do not forget to update your HIPAA compliance and other governing manuals to reflect the changes.

Regardless of how you store your information, sooner or later, the time comes for the data to be destroyed. Shredding is the most common solution for paper records. In-house shredding using a small business machine can be expensive because it requires staff time, and the machines tend to break. Commercial grade shredders are available. It is worth comparing the costs of these options to the cost of hiring a reputable document destruction company. Often the costs of outsourcing are comparable to those of in-house shredding, and the professionals provide documentation that your documents have been destroyed.

Getting rid of electronic data is more challenging than people realize. A plethora of computer programs and computer services companies purport to "wipe" your electronic data completely off of your storage devices. These claims can be overstated. For every company that purports to "wipe" the data, there is another that will restore that same device. When it comes to destroying electronic data, the safest thing to do is to destroy the hardware.

Relationships With Banks

Although business banking and personal banking have a lot in common, they differ in several important ways. Banks offer a range of services, products, and options for their business customers, including various types of savings, checking, and other accounts in which to keep your business's money. They also offer several types of loans to credit-worthy companies, each with its own unique features.

THE BUSINESS OF BANKING AND FINANCE

To begin a business banking relationship, you must, of course, have a business. From a banker's perspective, this means that, at a minimum, you must register a Taxpayer Identification Number (TIN) with the Internal Revenue Service (IRS). Banks and other financial institutions will not do business with a prospective customer who does not have a TIN.

One way around this requirement is to use your Social Security Number (SSN) as a numerical identifier instead of a business TIN. Because using your SSN may create an undesirable linkage between your business assets and your personal assets, consult with an Attorney before doing so. At the bottom line, Healthcare Entrepreneurs are well-advised to obtain a TIN and title their banking accounts in their company's name.

First, remember that you can work with more than one bank. Many professionals select a bank because it is conveniently located. Although it is certainly easier to make deposits at a bank down the block than a bank across town, convenience is not the only consideration when selecting a bank. Banks pay and charge different fees and offer various services. The convenience of banking nearby may be offset by the cost of their fees.

Nor should you necessarily choose a bank because it offers a particularly attractive interest rate, or perks such as free checking. These offerings, albeit desirable, tend to be transient. Different banks may offer services that can bring more long-term value to your practice. For example, consider which will serve you best: (1) a bank that charges a lot for a line of credit but offers free checking or (2) a bank that provides its business customers with a line of credit at a single point above the prime interest rate. The answer will vary from practice to practice, and it will change from time to time.

Understanding Banking Fees

Overdraft fees are the fees banks charge when a check is presented without sufficient funds in the customer's account to cover the check. If not managed, these fees can add up quickly. Before selecting a bank or a type of checking account, negotiate overdraft protection and some forgiveness or reduction of the overdraft fees. Such negotiations may be easier with a small local bank than a large regional or national bank.

Some banks will waive overdraft charges and agree to cover overdrafts for businesses with a good credit track record and sizable deposits. Other banks take a more cautious approach and will ask you to maintain a credit card or line of credit that will fund the payment of checks that cannot be fully paid from the funds in your checking account. When your balance is insufficient to pay an incoming check, the bank uses your credit card or line of credit to loan you the money needed to honor the check. These monies should be repaid as soon as possible.

Some banks charge hefty fees when a check from a patient or other payer is deposited but bounces. These fees should be passed on to the patient or payer who failed to cover the check. The agreement to pay a fee when a check does not clear the bank should be part of your patient agreement and should be detailed in your policies and procedures manual. Since there are costs associated with processing bounced checks, the fee you charge should exceed the fee the bank charges you.

Cash flow, which is the balance between the inflow and outflow of money, is always a consideration when operating a business of any sort. As an industry, healthcare presents all kinds of unique cash flow problems. For example, insurance companies, including federal payers such as Medicare, can delay payments by weeks or months without warning. Your creditors are not likely to accept the explanation that "Medicare is slow in paying claims this month" when it comes time for you to pay their bills. Therefore, access to lines of credit and cash reserves is essential to operating a healthy, stress-free practice.

The savvy Healthcare Entrepreneur always has a plan for surviving a cash flow crisis. Those who fail to have such a plan may find themselves paying hefty late payment fees and interest charges and diminishing their credit score while they wait for the cash needed to pay bills to start flowing again.

When bills outweigh the available income, a negative cash flow is created. To protect against problems created by a negative cash flow, keep a substantial amount of Cash On Hand (COH) in an easily accessible form, such as a savings or money market account. How much COH your company will need and in what form you keep it depends on your practice. Some practices keep enough COH to pay predictable expenses for one, three, or six months, and some even longer. Putting this money in stocks and other fluctuating investments is possible, but doing so risks having to sell the stocks at a loss when you need the cash. This money should be kept in an interest-bearing account from which funds can be quickly withdrawn without penalty.

Some Healthcare Entrepreneurs avoid keeping cash reserves on hand in their practice and choose instead to take money out of the practice as soon as possible. When the business needs cash to cover a loss or a temporary cash-flow problem, they personally lend the company the needed funds. Although occasionally circumstances make this a financially wise choice, for most businesses, this is a mistake for several reasons, including the muddying of the boundary between owner and business. The prudent Healthcare Entrepreneur works with an Accountant to set up plans for withdrawing unneeded cash from the business and for ensuring that cash is available when needed without loss of the boundary between owner and business.

For Healthcare Entrepreneurs who choose to rely on personal funds to cover cash shortfalls and other unusual expenses, it is wise to treat each of those transactions as if it were a loan between two unrelated entities. A formal loan agreement should be drawn up and signed, even if the lender and the recipient are the same individual. One signature represents the signer as lender and the second signature represents the signer as an officer of the practice. The loan document should specify the rate of interest, terms of repayment, the term of the loan, and remedies for failure to repay.

Many banks are willing to share loan forms with customers. Similar forms are available from Attorneys or can be downloaded as sample forms from the internet.

Choosing a Checking Account

Whether you pay your bills online or by paper check, your practice will need to have a business checking account. If you are in a partnership, you must determine who should have signature powers with which to authorize negotiable checks. In some partnerships, checks can be signed by a single designated partner or any one of the partners; in others, concurrent signatures from two or more of the partners, officers, or executives of the company are required.

Be aware that so-called "free" checking accounts often have hidden costs. Banks that offer such accounts often charge hefty fees for overdrafts and bounced checks and require a minimum balance. In practical terms, maintaining a minimum balance means that you will have money sitting in the account earning little or no interest.

A quick calculation can tell you whether you would be better off leaving the minimum balance sitting idle or investing that money and paying a monthly fee for the account. Simply take the rate of gains for a major stock index such as the Dow Jones Average or any other estimate of earnings from the sort of investment you might make and multiply that rate times the minimum required balance. If the result is greater than the amount saved with supposedly free checking, you might want to switch to a checking account that does not require a minimum balance.

Using Sweep Accounts

Because accessible cash is vital in any business, many practices keep all their cash in their checking account(s) so money is always available for paying bills. The cost of taking this approach is the loss of profits from investment opportunities.

Many banks offer sweep accounts to valued customers who tend to leave a sizable balance in a non-interest-bearing checking account. When unused cash sits in such accounts, it is idle. Sweep accounts are designed to "sweep" that money into an investment account, such as a money market account, at the end of each business day and then sweep the same money back into a usable account, such as a checking account, the next morning. This allows the business owner to earn interest on the cash while still having the cash in a liquid enough form to pay bills as needed. The advantage for the bank is that the money is left in the bank over an extended period of time.

It is wise to check the "average daily balance" portion of your checking and savings account statements to see how much money you typically leave in the bank. If the amount is sizable, it is worth talking to your banker about instituting a sweep account. If your bank doesn't offer sweep accounts, consider switching to a bank that offers that option.

Making Deposits

For a growing number of practices, making trips to the bank is becoming a thing of the past. Payments from third-party payers are often transferred electronically, as are payments made by patients using credit cards. Even paper checks can now be deposited in the bank electronically. Many banks offer the option of using check readers, which scan checks from your office into the bank account of your choosing. With rare exceptions, there are fees and expenses associated with using this technology.

Check readers cannot process cash; however, there are several ways to handle cash without losing time going to the bank. One option is to set a no-cash-accepted policy. Such a policy has the additional advantage of reducing the likelihood of theft. Of course, it also increases the likelihood that some patients will have to be billed for fees that would have been paid at the check-in window at the time services were rendered.

Another option is to have all cash payments transferred to an owner of the practice, who immediately compensates the practice with a personal check in the amount of the cash received. This check can then be deposited electronically.

Paying Bills Online

Paying bills can be a time-consuming, costly task. Most banks and many vendors offer the option of paying bills online. Especially when this option is paired with electronic statements from your vendors, paying bills online can save time, as well as the costs associated with mailing paper checks. Banks differ in how they charge for this service; some banks have restrictions on which bills you can pay online. It is worth asking your banker to provide this service for free in exchange for your business or, at least, to discount or forego some of the fees associated with online bill paying.

LOANS AND OTHER FORMS OF CREDIT

Lines of Credit

Lines of Credit (LOCs) are a source of cash for covering shortfalls and come in many forms. Financial experts like to point out that home equity lines of credit (HELOCs) bring a tax advantage because interest paid on the LOC is treated as interest on a home mortgage when it comes time to pay federal income tax.

Although it is certainly desirable to capture that savings, there are rules governing the use of money drawn from HELOCs that must be respected. Doing so also blurs the line between the business and the owner whose home is the collateral for the HELOC. This may weaken or breach some or all of the liability protection that ostensibly is present when the boundaries between an incorporated business and its owner are consistently respected.

Another type of LOC is based solely on the signature of the owner or authorized officers of a credit-worthy business. Aptly referred to as "Signature Loans," these LOCs are an essential business resource. When cash flow is poor, as it can be when payers suddenly slow down their payments in response to their own cash flow, the Signature Loan allows the business owner to continue to pay bills and meet payroll.

There are some risks and drawbacks, however. For example, many of these LOCs require the owner to cosign the loan documents, thus shifting risk and liability to the owner's personal assets. In addition, because the lender is in the business of loaning money, many are happy to accept monthly payments that do little or nothing to whittle down the principal amount borrowed. If not managed properly, this can result in a business getting too deeply into debt to be stable. Before you apply for a loan of any sort for your business, review your budget and revise it as necessary to make sure the loan can be repaid within a reasonable time.

Businesses that have had some problems with credit in the past or those that are too new to qualify for a signature loan often can still get a routine business LOC, which functions much like a signature LOC. The key difference is that the business LOC requires collateral as backing for it. The collateral can be in any mutually agreeable form, including the equipment or Accounts Receivable owned by the practice.

In addition to the interest charged on money borrowed, some LOCs charge fees such as initiation fees, application fees, and renewal fees. When selecting a bank with which to conduct your daily business, ask about and negotiate these fees. A bank that is interested in attracting your business may be more willing to waive or reduce these fees than a bank that you first approach as a stranger in need.

Business Term Loans

A business may need or want to borrow money to fund its start-up or growth, buy new equipment, or expand into other areas. Business Term Loans (BTLs) are a traditional means of borrowing for such situations.

Before securing a loan, estimate how the money you spend benefits your business. It makes little sense to purchase a piece of equipment unless you have a reasonable expectation that the equipment will pay for itself and begin to generate profits in a reasonable time frame. The estimate should include the expenses associated with paying off the loans, including the principal amount of the loan, interest, and any fees. The prudent Healthcare Entrepreneur also compares the estimated profits that might be derived from the purchase with the profits that might be generated if the money were spent in other ways.

When it comes to expensive equipment, many sales companies offer financing. In some cases, the financing option deserves consideration, but remember that these companies are seldom in the business of lending money. Instead, they serve as a "middle-man" between a buyer and a lender or they actually do loan money to the buyer and then quickly sell the loan to a company that invests in financial obligations. Either way, the middle-man will take a profit, which often means the cost to the borrower goes up. Carefully read *all* loan documents, especially those from equipment sales companies. Never sign an agreement that you cannot understand and live with comfortably.

Credit Card Account Management

Choosing the right credit card(s), whether from a bank or other financial institution, can be a complex process. Many Healthcare Entrepreneurs subscribe to credit cards that are used strictly for business expenses. Doing so saves time and maintains the boundaries between their businesses and their personal lives. Having separate credit cards also promotes expedient bookkeeping and avoids the need to review expenditures to determine whether they were made on behalf of the business or the individual.

Other professionals, citing factors such as convenience and the desire to accumulate reward points, use the same credit card for both business and personal purchases, even though it means they must review each charge later. This approach also requires that the account from which the credit card bill is paid be appropriately reimbursed for one type of expense or the other. For example, if a personal card is used for all transactions and the bill for purchases made on that card is paid from the professional's personal bank account, the practice must reimburse the professional for payments attributable to the business.

CHAPTER 4

Sales, Marketing, Branding And Community Relations

Becoming a successful Healthcare Entrepreneur requires objectivity and clear thinking. Sometimes, this means re-visiting and re-considering ideas that influence our behaviors but about which we haven't given much thought.

For example, in this age of aggressive online sales (witness the pop-up ads we get the day after we search for a product), and aggressive marketing (candidates can't successfully run for office without using robocalls), the terms "sales," "marketing," and "branding" have taken on negative connotations.

In fact, each is a key element of any successful economy and each is an important tool for a prosperous business. Each can and should be implemented in ways that are professional, respectful, and effective. It's important to keep an open, objective mind.

MARKETING IS NOT SALES

Although they are sometimes paired, marketing and sales are two separate and distinct functions. *Marketing* is the process of promoting awareness of a product, service, or brand. An example is the banners a sports medicine group hangs on the fence at every little league and high school playing field in their region. *Selling* is the process of convincing someone to actually buy a product or service. Often, this comes in the form of addressing the prospective patient's concerns about the treatment or service they are considering. An example of selling is the cosmetic surgeon's recounting of how quickly their patients are back to their daily routines.

Each function obviously influences the other, and for this reason, they are sometimes housed together in an organization. Unfortunately, many professionals confuse the two functions and end up doing both ineffectively or not doing them at all.

Marketing Activities

Marketing activities are designed to raise awareness of a specific service, treatment, brand, or type of product or service such as holistic medicine. Marketing campaigns capture the consumer's attention through a marketing medium such as the internet, newspaper ads, church bulletins, banners, and sponsorships at charity events.

The most effective professional healthcare marketing efforts are educational in nature and are focused on services or treatments. Examples include marketing campaigns extolling the benefits of robotic surgery, ocular lens implants, or psychotherapy. In professional marketing, you are not competing with your colleagues because you are promoting services they also promote. Marketing yourself is the unavoidable and desirable side-effect of having your business, your name, and your image associated with the educational piece.

Educational marketing stands in contrast to marketing efforts from other non-healthcare professions in which marketing efforts, sometimes of necessity, focus on convincing potential consumers they should employ a particular professional or company. These are "branding" campaigns. The legal profession uses branding and, less often, general marketing.

It is relatively rare for Attorneys to be able to use educational marketing to promote a new service since relatively few new services emerge in law. An exception was the emergence of "collaborative family law" in which Attorneys help marital partners negotiate the terms of their divorce without resorting to litigation. Practitioners who trained in and offered this service were able to switch from branding campaigns with themes like "hire me, I am better than the rest" to marketing campaigns focused on messages such as "you can have divorce without war." Those that made the marketing shift immediately gained prominence by demonstrating their knowledge of a new and desirable service.

Healthcare Entrepreneurs always stay ahead of the game by simply keeping abreast of the latest research, technologies, and methodologies for their specialty. After learning about something new that has clinical value, the successful Healthcare Entrepreneur also considers how to market what they have learned.

Most marketing campaigns require repeated exposure of their message over time. Rarely is a single exposure enough to imprint a brand or service in a consumer or referral source's mind. So, when a novice Healthcare Entrepreneur drops off brochures at a potential referral source's office, that marketing effort is unlikely to bear much fruit without repeat visits and other reminders necessary to prime the pump with that referral source.

When done thoughtfully and well, marketing can have a rapid impact because most consumers base their decisions on impressions and subjective reactions rather than facts. The more your marketing campaign saturates its target audience, the more likely a prospective patient will think of you if and when they need services. That's why swag — items like pens and T-shirts bearing your practice's logo — are effective marketing tools.

Marketing for Healthcare Entrepreneurs

Some professional marketing lends itself better to one-to-one marketing rather than marketing to groups or communities. Successful personal marketing by a Healthcare Entrepreneur involves building enough of a relationship with referral sources and patients that they become justifiably comfortable with you. The feeling may arise from personal qualities you display, your impressive credentials, your outstanding achievements, things you and another person have in common, or simply getting to know each other over time. Building relationships at this level is a key to successful marketing.

When marketing, it is essential to take time to visit with your prospective referral source or other business associate. Learn about the other person and let the other person learn about you. Although it is important for you to carry your share of the conversation, let the other person lead the way. When other people feel heard by you, they will be more attentive to what you have to say. Ideally, they have shared information that allows you to make the points you want to make in ways that tie into the prospect's interests and needs.

Learn about the prospect's needs, interests, goals, and preferences. Some of this information can be gleaned from an internet search prior to the meeting; most can be determined by asking the right questions and listening to your prospect's answers. This is an important step in both marketing and sales.

Some of your marketing efforts will benefit your competitors because as you market your own services, you are marketing those of your entire profession. For this reason, it is essential to know what differentiates you from your competitors. As soon as your prospect shows signs of being sold on the service in general, you, as an effective salesperson, should guide their attention to your own unique features.

> **TIP:** While it is common to use business lunches and other activities to build relationships, consider the question of who picks up the tab. Paying for a lavish meal while meeting with someone who does, or may in the future, make referrals might be construed as an inducement to make those referrals.

For example, once an Occupational Therapist has interested a Gerontologist in the benefits of occupational therapy for homebound patients, the Occupational Therapist should highlight features that make their practice unique such as specialization in the needs of the elderly, ease of scheduling, the convenience of location, and so on.

Sales Activities

Sales activities are targeted toward getting people to buy what you are selling. The focus here is on completing a business transaction between a business owner or representative and a customer. Consider, for example, two Chiropractors who often recommend yoga and muscle stretching to their patients, emphasizing the health benefits of such activities. Their recommendation is a marketing activity designed to increase patient awareness of a beneficial service.

But, if one of the Chiropractors offers yoga classes as part of their practice and encourages their patients to sign up for the classes, this is a sales activity that comes on the heels of the marketing effort inherent in recommending the health benefits of the service.

One component of the sales process involves what salespeople call "overcoming objections." A potential buyer or referral source may not have voiced any objections aloud; however, by our nature, people are always screening information for "the catch" or problem with whatever is being proposed or discussed. Even when your prospect is intrigued by what you have to say, their internal voice may warn them against moving too quickly or deviating from their current way of doing things. One of the many ways that salespeople help overcome objections is by anticipating likely objections and addressing them before they are even spoken.

Anyone who has purchased a car has likely heard a salesperson say, "Excuse me for a moment. I am going to talk to my finance manager to see if I can get you a better deal." The salesperson might even "sweeten the deal" by not charging for an accessory that the customer previously said he or she would like to have. With either of those simple statements, the salesperson attempts to overcome and pre-empt the buyer's objections to pricing.

For the most part, car sales techniques are not recommended for those attempting to sell professional services. For example, using financial incentives to entice a professional prospect can be illegal and is likely to backfire. On the other hand, many of the principles underlying commodities sales can also play a role in professional marketing. One example is changing the prospect's perception of the risk-to-reward ratio. In many businesses, this can be accomplished by reducing the perceived risk by putting items on sale. In professional marketing, this is ill-advised. Instead, the risk-to-reward ratio is managed by adding to the reward. A Dietician might accomplish this by co-hosting cooking classes with a local Restauranteur at their co-hosts restaurant, for example.

As you talk to prospects, listen for what they see as the potential risks and rewards of working with you. Make it a point to address the risks and enhance the rewards. For example, a Healthcare Entrepreneur who does not accept insurance should make that fact clear, all the while emphasizing advantages such as more time with each patient that comes with a fee-for-service practice model.

"Closing the sale" is used to describe the successful culmination of a sales effort. It involves a clearly stated agreement as to what each person will do and when. Broad, general agreements bode poorly for future business transactions. Consider the difference between the prospect who says, "I will be happy to send a few patients your way," and the prospect who says, "Let's do this. I will send you the next two cases I see. After that, we can look at how things went with those cases."

Professional sales rarely involve a "hard" sell or any form of pressure tactic. The exception is when a Healthcare Entrepreneur is competing for a contract with a large corporation or other business entity. In virtually all other circumstances, Healthcare Entrepreneurs rely on the merits of what they are offering, combined with frequent reminders that their services are available and have value.

NETWORKING AND COMMUNITY RELATIONS

Healthcare Entrepreneurs start their practices from many different postures. Some start their practices in their hometowns, where they are well known and already well networked; others stay in the vicinity in which they trained, where they have some roots and connections. Still others move someplace they have never lived, where they know few if any people and must establish new relationships with colleagues, referral sources, and the community at large. Successful sales and marketing depend heavily on building and maintaining networks throughout the community in which you practice.

Regardless of where you are beginning, it is essential to develop the relationships you need to build and sustain your business. Some of those relationships will be built on a one-to-one basis; others will be built naturally with relatively little effort in small groups such as professional societies, hospital staffs, religious congregations, and recreational events.

Effective Healthcare Entrepreneurs do not stop there. They also build relationships with the community at large. One way to accomplish this is by accepting leadership positions in organizations that can help rapidly and widely expand the Healthcare Entrepreneur's networks. These positions serve as a branding tool. The time spent is the fee for the marketing. As with any fee, the cost–benefit ratio should be reassessed periodically.

REPUTATION MANAGEMENT

Although the times are changing, most professionals' reputations are tied to their personal names. However, the reputations of most businesses are also associated with the business's name and the names of its products or services. Cleaning up a public relations problem is easier for a named business than it is for a healthcare professional whose personal name has been besmudged.

Healthcare Entrepreneurs tend to handle adverse publicity differently than business owners in other fields. Their time and other resources are more limited than those of larger businesses. Time spent responding to patient complaints and bad press is time away from providing the services that generate the money needed to run the practice. Deciding whether and how to manage bad press boils down to dollars and cents. Emotional factors such as the desire to "clear my good name" muddy thinking and can lead to regrettable choices. When faced with negative press, the prudent Healthcare Entrepreneur takes several steps before deciding whether to get caught up in the perceived problem.

First, to the extent possible, stop the problem; don't add fuel to the fire. Second, perform a cost–benefit analysis to determine whether the potential for financial damage justifies the cost of responding. Third, consult a public relations expert who can review your cost–benefit analysis, point out missed considerations, and, if need be, implement strategies to respond to the threat successfully.

Although most public relations problems eventually lose steam and die down, these problems live in perpetuity on the internet. Innumerable websites purport to offer web surfers valuable information about how each healthcare professional performs in the eyes of those who take the time to post opinions and ratings. Of course, these ratings are spurious and are likely to be more heavily loaded with the discontent of unhappy consumers in need of some catharsis than the praise of happy patients who are willing to take the time to offer their opinions.

Regardless of their validity and accuracy, online ratings do influence consumer opinions and consumer choices, so it is worthwhile to keep your online image clean. Prevention is, perhaps, the best weapon. Within the bounds of professional ethics, campaigns to encourage patients to share their positive experiences online can help tilt your ratings. When the damage is already done, there are professionals who will, for a fee, clean up your image on the web.

You can err in the rush to address negative press. For example, it can be a mistake to respond to criticism publicly; doing so keeps the focus on the bad press and risks violations of confidentiality. It is also a mistake to post your own ratings using pseudonyms. Besides being dishonest, these postings tend to come off sounding stilted and "canned."

Some bad press is built into the healthcare system in America. For example, payers, including federal government payers, sponsor aggressive campaigns to encourage patients to ferret out and report fraud and abuse by healthcare providers. These campaigns can leave the public with the impression that no one in the healthcare industry can be trusted.

The private insurance sector uses industry-specific jargon that implies that health-care providers are unscrupulous. Terms such as "not medically necessary" and "charges above the usual and customary" are used to describe reasonable bills and fees that are not covered or not well covered by a given insurance plan. The impli-cation of such terms is that healthcare professionals routinely take advantage of the patients to line their own pockets.

When patients call their insurance company to complain about a denied claim, the person to whom they speak is charged with calming the patient down and making sure the patient, who, after all, is the insurance company's customer, leaves the call feeling good about the company. Sometimes this is done by blame shifting. For example, consider the insurance company representative who explained a denied claim by telling their customer that the claim would have been paid had the doctor "billed the correct code." The patient is left with the belief that the doctor's error left them, the patient, with an avoidable bill when, in fact, the doctor billed honestly and correctly, but the insurance policy does not cover the code that was billed.

The savvy Healthcare Entrepreneur avoids the temptation to manage these slurs on their reputation by fighting fire with fire. Speaking badly of the source of mis-information is more likely to leave the patients feeling befuddled than it is to help calm the patient and restore goodwill.

Two other strategies are more effective here. First, always maintain a positive relationship with your patients. Even during brief visits with patients you seldom see, it is possible to engage the patient in a relationship by expressing an interest in something that is important to them beyond their health. Some Healthcare Entre-preneurs keep notes about things like their patients' hobbies and children's names so that they can engage the patient in brief, relationship-building conversations.

Education is another effective way to help a patient who has been misinformed or misled by others. Ideally, education starts early. For example, printed material in the waiting room can help educate patients that "not medically necessary" means "not covered by your insurance policy" rather than "not an important component of your care." Additional education can occur as patients use services, such as advising patients in advance when a procedure they believe will be covered by their insurance is not, in your experience, typically covered under this patient's unique circumstance. When necessary, education can also be provided later by inviting an upset patient in to discuss, perhaps with a staff member, why the coding you used was the only honest coding available.

Savvy Healthcare Entrepreneurs know there are plenty of other competent professionals in their field, so they manage their reputation, maintain their personal and professional networks, and look for opportunities to market their valuable services.

Patient Relations

Your relationships with your patients and others are a vital asset of your practice. The quality of those relationships influences virtually every aspect of your business. Healthcare Entrepreneurs attend to and nourish their relationships in general and their relationships with patients in particular. Patients are your responsibility, your potentially best spokesperson, and your source of bread and butter all at once.

UNDERSTANDING YOUR CUSTOMERS AND CONSTITUENTS

In most nonhealthcare businesses, the question "Who is the customer?" is easily answered. For a company that sells merchandise, the customer is the person or entity that buys the goods being sold. When a big-box electronics store buys computers from a manufacturer, the store becomes that manufacturer's customer. When the store sells those same computers to an individual, that individual becomes the store's customer. The store will do its best to meet the customer's needs. On the other hand, from the manufacturer's perspective, the store's customers are "end-users," not customers. The manufacturer and the end-users do not have a relationship.

Things are not so straightforward in most healthcare practices. There is plenty of room to debate the question of who the customer is. The presumptive answer is usually "The patient is the customer." This answer clearly is correct in some respects, but it is lacking in others. Health insurers and other third-party payers might be regarded as customers when they pay for a service. With more than one customer having a stake in almost every transaction, Healthcare Entrepreneurs must carefully consider their duties to each.

In healthcare, relationships are more complex and ambiguous than they are in most other industries. This is particularly true when insurance companies and other third-party payers are involved. A number of dyads — relationships between two or more people or businesses —link together to form a complex chain. The relationships look like those illustrated in Figure 1, with four parties forming six dyads, thus creating conflicts of interest.

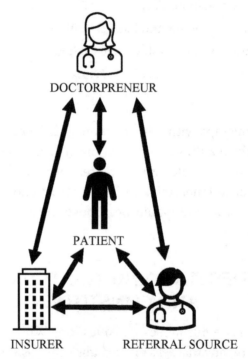

Figure 1. Six Relationships Among Four Entities

As Figure 1 shows, when third-party payers are involved, as many as six relationships are at play in a simple patient care encounter. Only three of the relationships include the patient directly: the relationship of the patient to the insurance company, the relationship of the patient to the referral source, and the relationship of the patient to the healthcare professional who actually renders services. Even with just these three relationships, things have already become far more complicated and potentially more conflictual than they would be in a simple relationship between patient and healthcare professional.

With a few exceptions, when managed health insurance is involved, three additional relationships come into play. Each of the six dyads formed has its own unique contracts and agreements that guide them and impact the other five dyads.

For example, many insurance companies or other managed care entities use contracts that limit the pool of referral sources to "preferred providers" or some other limited subset of the available referral options. This often puts the treating professional in the position of either violating their contract with the insurance company or betraying their obligation to a patient when a better referral could be made outside of the approved pool. Should a patient be referred to the most competent specialist available or to a specialist approved by the patient's insurance company, even if that person is not the best choice?

When you define your patient as your customer, you will make decisions that protect the customer, even when doing so might create a problem in the relationship you or your customer have with an insurance company. Conversely, if you define your customer as the insurance company, you are more likely to make decisions that favor the insurance company. When it comes time to resolve these ethical dilemmas, it is helpful for Healthcare Entrepreneurs to put aside the term *customers* and think in terms of *constituents*.

Constituents help make up the whole of your practice. They are people or businesses that count on you to represent their best interests. This change in mindset and verbiage helps brings into focus the true essence of each of the relationships you as a Healthcare Entrepreneur have with each of several groups with which you conduct business.

At the bottom line, Healthcare Entrepreneurs, much like CEOs in other industries, must balance the competing needs of their various constituencies when making decisions. Defining who your constituents are helps you to take each one's needs and perspectives into account. It also guides important business decisions, such as where to market, to whom to market, as well as which segments of the market should be sought and which should be avoided.

PATIENT RETENTION: A PATIENT'S-EYE VIEW OF YOUR PRACTICE

Your relationship with a patient begins long before your first actual contact with that patient. The relationship begins as soon as the patient becomes aware of your practice. A person who learns of your practice by scanning their insurance company's directory or an internet listing will approach you in a different way than a person who was told by a trusted primary care physician that you are the best in your field. So, although there is a tendency to lump patients together into one big category, remember that each patient or prospective patient is a unique person with unique perspectives and expectations.

For these reasons, it is important to ask your referral sources to be thoughtful about what they say to the patient when making a referral. It is also important to make sure that your marketing and advertising materials send the kind of message that will ensure that your relationship with a patient begins on a positive note. Advertisements and endorsements from referral sources should be encouraging and hopeful without creating unrealistic expectations. Your relationship with a new patient who was told you are "the best in town" may be quite different than if that patient had been told you are "very well trained and experienced."

The first interaction between two people has a deep, long-lasting impact on their relationship over the long term. Stated simply, first impressions count, so it is important that telephone calls, emails, and other types of communication be answered promptly. For the same reason, it is important that the front office staff be trained to represent your practice in the best possible way. A sunny disposition is more powerful than a catchy slogan when it comes to attracting and retaining patients. Your staff must be trained regarding behaviors that make your practice inviting.

Each practice has its own "personality." Some practices prefer to make personal connections with their patients; others prefer to keep things formal and business-like. Each type of system and every variation has its advantages and disadvantages. At a minimum, it is helpful to establish the tone of the relationship at the outset of the first contact. Consider the difference between a phone call that is answered with the greeting "Anderson Cardiology" versus the greeting "Thank you for calling Anderson Cardiology. This is Jack. How may I help you today?"

TIP: Office staff attitudes and dispositions tend to mirror those of their bosses. Always model the attitudes and behaviors you want to see in your staff.

Your building and office space also influence how your patients will relate to you. Offices that are messy or look neglected may cause unease in patients who expect a professional office to be clean, neat, organized, and well-appointed. As they realign their expectations to match their experience, even if stereotyped, patients will, without thinking much about it, assign all sorts of value judgments to you, the professional they have yet to meet.

Consider how you feel when you first enter a well-maintained but functionally furnished office. Then consider how you feel when you first enter an office that has soothing, inviting features such as plants and decorative fountains. Those who want to establish a high-volume practice may choose to set up a white-walled office lined with functional waiting room chairs to get patients in the mindset of taking care of business efficiently. Those who are interested in increasing the proportion of their patients who eschew insurance and pay full fee will have to invest in a more inviting environment.

Trust is an essential component of any relationship, especially the relationship between a healthcare professional and a patient. Unfortunately, trust can be more easily damaged than sustained. Although most people can forgive minor violations of trust, even those can add up and take their toll. Trust is diminished when people fail to do what they say, even when the failure is understandable. For example, when a professional arrives late for an appointment, the professional's credibility is diminished regardless of the reason for the tardiness. Delivering on promises spoken or implied is an invaluable component of any effort to build a positive patient experience in your office.

A common patient complaint involves the quantity of paperwork that is required at a first visit. Regulatory compliance and liability management considerations underlie much of the paperwork; however, when a form or an item on a form can be eliminated, do so. Patient portals and kiosks that are available in many practice management and EMR programs allow patients to complete the paperwork before arriving for an appointment. The amount of effort is the same, but the negative effects are muted.

Another way to minimize intake paperwork is to have a member of the support staff meet with the patient prior to the appointment to obtain some of the needed information in a conversational manner. While costly, this approach can have a positive effect on the patient's overall experience and help meet the practice's need for essential information.

TIP: Offer older patients forms printed in 20 point type. They will appreciate it.

Most patients leave a healthcare professional's office retaining only a fraction of what they were told. Patients appreciate receiving written information about key points, such as their diagnosis, medication regimens, schedule of next steps to follow, and instructions for those steps. Follow-up calls from a member of the staff, while expensive, go a long way toward ensuring compliance and patient loyalty.

TIP: Send billing reminders early in the week to maximize the likelihood of payment.

One easy way to bruise or damage an otherwise positive relationship with a patient is to leave the patient feeling stuck with a question or a problem related to billing. Such a question or problem causes the patient stress. The longer a patient is in that state of stress, the harder it will be to assuage the patient's concerns. Prompt resolution of problems and concerns is part of the best practices.

Insurers often send patients a copy of the Explanation of Benefits (EOB) for every service the patient receives. If the EOB is well-organized, the patient should be able to understand the benefits. Unfortunately, many payers use a confusing format for the EOB.

> **TIP:** Posting the answers to commonly asked billing questions on your website helps reduce the time spent answering those questions by phone. Recorded responses can also be played when patients are placed on hold while waiting to speak to billing personnel.

Helping patients understand their EOB helps build relationships while reducing misunderstandings and conflict. Even seasoned professionals sometimes must think long and hard to interpret and understand what many EOBs mean. A patient who is unfamiliar with how to interpret EOBs may misconstrue the information and attribute their problems to the treating professional. For example, the codes and explanations used when a claim is rejected strongly imply that the professional did something wrong or, in many cases, something unethical, such as charging more than is "usual and customary." This phrase implies that the Healthcare Entrepreneur is attempting to overcharge their patient. Consequently, when a patient calls to question a bill, it is likely with a negative predisposition. The longer a patient holds onto this belief, the more deep-seated and intractable their resentments will become. It is important for patients to have ready access to a trained staff member who can help answer questions and explain their bills. See Table 7 for examples of misleading terms.

> **TIP:** Billing inquiries can be handled much more efficiently when the person replying to the inquiry knows what the caller's concerns are and has time to research the concern. A billing help line on which messages can be recorded can add efficiency, without leaving the patient in distress for any longer than necessary. Consider this script:
>
> "Hello, you have reached Sue in the billing office at the Lucrative Practice Institute. Although I cannot answer the phone right now, I do try to respond to billing inquiries within eight business hours of when an email or voice-mail message is

received. For the fastest service, please consider emailing your question to Billing@ LucrativePractices.com or, if you would prefer, after the tone please state your question, the action you would like me to take, your name, your return phone number, and convenient times that I can call you back."

TABLE 7. Some Misleading Terms That Confuse Patients

1. *"Not medically necessary"* is often used to describe a service that either is not covered or is explicitly excluded in the patient's unique insurance policy. The same service may be covered by the same carrier under a different plan.
2. *"Usual and customary fees"* are the values assigned by the payer for a given service without much regard for factors such as the cost of rendering the service or the actual value of the service in the open market.
3. *"Provider"* is a term the insurance industry uses to lump all professionals into one grouping, implying that, like any piece of equipment or purveyor of common goods, healthcare professionals are interchangeable thus diminishing the doctor-patient relationship.
4. *"Member"* is an inviting term the insurance industry uses to refer to their customers. Membership imparts a subtle sense of affiliation and affinity to the insurer. So, when a "member" is told by their insurer that the professional's fee is too high, they will be more likely to side with the company of which they are a "member."

On the other side of the coin, the cost of paying someone to answer billing questions is just that, a cost. There is no way to recoup that expense. Thus, each Healthcare Entrepreneur must decide which of two primary options best suits the practice's model and needs. On the one hand, patient satisfaction can be enhanced by paying a patient advocate to help with things like billing questions. On the other hand, professionals who want to maximize profits and are willing to alienate a few patients to do so can take a play from the insurance industry's playbook by putting non-reimbursable services such as billing inquiries on hold until someone gets around to them.

Among the variables that cause patient dissatisfaction is the sense that the treating professional does not care about them or their opinions. An inexpensive yet effective way to enhance satisfaction is to request patient feedback after every visit. Options range from online forms to postage-paid postcards.

Although most patients will not take the time to give feedback, those who would otherwise quietly stew are more likely to calm down if they have a way to vent. Those who might otherwise put disparaging feedback on any of the innumerable "rate your professional" internet sites might forego doing so if they know their feedback will be heard or read by the professional about whom they have concerns. An acknowledgment that the feedback was received, is appreciated, and will be taken into account in the future can convert an irate patient into a returning patient.

KEEPING PATIENTS INFORMED – NO SURPRISES

It is not uncommon for patients to expect that all services recommended or offered by a licensed professional will be covered by their insurance policy. This expectation is unrealistic because most policies specify a limited number of covered services and a number of services that are explicitly not covered.

When a recommended service is not covered by insurance, the patient must decide whether to pay for it out of pocket or forego the recommended procedure(s). When this dilemma occurs in the case of a Medicare beneficiary, the Healthcare Entrepreneur is required to review the circumstances with the patient and obtain a signed Advanced Beneficiary Notice of Noncoverage (ABN) before accepting payment from the patient. Such steps often are not required if the patient is covered by a commercial insurance policy, but whether or not it is required, the prudent Healthcare Entrepreneur will take the time to follow the same procedures. By forewarning patients of a forthcoming bill, the Healthcare Entrepreneur reduces the odds of nonpayment.

> **TIP:** Save time by downloading the Advanced Beneficiary Notice of Noncoverage (Form CMS-R-131) directly from the CMS website:
>
> www.cms.gov/Medicare/Medicare-General-Information/BNI/ABN.

MANAGING NO-SHOWS AND LATE CANCELLATIONS

Missed appointments can be among the most expensive costs of operating a practice. It costs money to schedule the patient, contact the patient (often repeatedly) to reschedule, and document the missed appointment. Missed appointments also mean missed earning opportunities. Stated simply, no-shows and cancellations are all cost and no revenue, so the management of missed appointments deserves extra attention.

To help discourage missed appointments, written patient agreements should include prominent language stating that the patient will be charged for missed appointments and late cancellations, and that such charges will not be billed to or paid for by insurance. The agreement should include a signature line for the incoming patient to indicate their acceptance of the responsibility to pay for missed appointments. Insurance contracts that prohibit charging for missed appointments should be renegotiated. Successful renegotiation ranges from eliminating the prohibition to increasing fees for services that are actually rendered in proportion to the predicted losses from the missed appointments.

Policies and procedures regarding collecting no-show and late cancellation fees should be managed like any other business procedure. That is, they should be based on the business interests of the practice. If the practice is well-established and thriving, it makes little sense to accept the costs of a no-show as an unreimbursed burden. On the other side of the coin, a new practitioner may choose to have a more forgiving policy in the service of bringing in and retaining new patients. Whatever policies and procedures are adopted, they should be clinically appropriate and uniformly enforced.

GAUGING PATIENT SATISFACTION

Feedback from patients can be among the most important pieces of information you can obtain about your practice. When appropriately collected, analyzed, and considered, your patients' thoughts and opinions can help improve efficiency, prevent liabilities, and guide marketing.

Too often, healthcare professionals eschew patient satisfaction surveys altogether. Those professionals who do ask their patients for input tend to rely on the same form with the same questions, year after year. Savvy Healthcare Entrepreneurs approach patient surveying with specific goals in mind. They focus on one or more particular aspects of their practice and revise their surveys accordingly.

When crafting items for a survey, ensure the items are worded in a way that invites honest, open input. Consider the difference between "True or False: The Receptionist was friendly" and "On a scale of 1 to 5, how comfortable were you while interacting with the Receptionist?" The first question limits the patient, while the second invites an open response and requires the patient to think back to the experience with your Receptionist.

When crafting a patient satisfaction survey, think through the entire customer experience, from what prompted them to contact you all the way through to discharge. Of course, you do not want to flood your patients with so many items that they race thoughtlessly through the form, so use multiple forms, each focused on different areas of interest to you and different components of the patient's experience. You can give different forms to different patients or switch from one form to another from time to time.

A patient's experience with your practice starts well before the first phone call; therefore, be sure to ask questions like, "How did you learn about us?" "What motivated you to choose this practice?" and "Whom can we thank for referring you to our practice?" Inquire about the experience each step of the way. Carefully worded items can reduce the temptation to overrate an item. Likewise, prefaces such as "We really want to do our best. Please think of anything, even little things, we could do to improve your experience" help promote truthful responses. See Checklist 3 for sample survey categories.

CHECKLIST 3

Patient Satisfaction Survey Categories

✓ Ease of access
✓ Responsiveness to inquiries
✓ Relationship with healthcare professionals
✓ Confidence in healthcare professionals
✓ Clarity of communications
✓ Physical plant
✓ Satisfaction with outcomes
✓ Clarity of billing
✓ Continuity of care
✓ Overall experience
✓ Likelihood of recommendation to others

AVOIDING MALPRACTICE CLAIMS AND LICENSING BOARD COMPLAINTS

A malpractice suit or licensing board complaint can suck the life out of a practice and the people who work in it. The costs of defending lawsuits and complaints go well beyond those measured in dollars. The toll is arguably greater when calculated in terms of demoralization, loss of self-confidence, negative public relations, and loss of employee loyalty.

Prevention is the key to managing malpractice complaints. Although it is hard to imagine a licensed professional intentionally committing an act or omission that would lead to a complaint or litigation, such acts and omissions occur more frequently than we may realize. No professional is "on their best game" all the time. Professionals who continue to render services when they are at a low ebb place themselves at a heightened risk of making mistakes, so systems must be in place to prevent such mistakes.

Nor is anyone able to unfailingly maintain a professional persona. Psychotherapists use the term "countertransference" to describe their emotional and behavioral responses to their patients. The patient who, even subtly, reminds you of someone else in your life sends cues to which you will naturally react. Sometimes the reactions are unwarranted and counterproductive. There are steps you can take, such as frequently using the patient's name and maintaining eye contact, to help minimize such reactions.

As a healthcare professional, you are in the business of taking care of people who often are not at their best. We know that people regress when they are ill, injured, scared, or grieving. Patients who are suffering can bring irrational expectations and heightened sensitivities into their relationships with those who are trying to help them. Sometimes this manifests as harsh words. Responding in kind simply invites trouble and puts the patient in charge of the tone of the interaction. Prudent Healthcare Entrepreneurs maintain control over the tenor of their office and the tone of their relationship with others. There is no value to getting into a squabble with a patient, even if they have hurt your feelings or offended you.

Nor is it often helpful to "correct" a patient's misperceptions or mistaken opinions. When people are corrected, they become defensive and begin to see the source of the correction as an adversary. Instead, when you think it is important to address a misperception or mistaken belief, do so by acknowledging the patient's perspective and then sharing your own. Stick to the facts so as to move the discussion out of the realms of emotions and opinions. Leave it to the patient to work out the differences.

One step toward preventing malpractice claims and complaints involves understanding some of the myths surrounding them. One common myth is that "it won't happen to me." Some may argue that this naive opinion is inherently arrogant. In fact, professional arrogance is a common thread in many patients' complaints. On the other side of the coin, the professional who approaches each patient as a potential litigant will miss the mark and increase the risk for error and the room for patient discontent. The savvy Healthcare Entrepreneur "assumes the best and prepares for the worst."

Professional arrogance comes in many forms. As discussed above, a belief that one professional is somehow so different from the rest of their colleagues that they will never be sued or aggrieved is one example. A close "cousin" is the belief that the professional's relationship with each patient is so special that the patient will hold the professional harmless regardless of what happens. True, many patients are more protective of professionals with whom they have a good rapport, but good rapport does not make the professional bulletproof. The line between arrogance and confidence can sometimes be thin.

Professional arrogance also comes into play when professionals, understandably trusting of their own informed opinions on a matter, are overly zealous in their efforts to drive a patient toward a specific decision. What may be the technically correct decision may not be the correct decision for that patient at that time. The prudent Healthcare Entrepreneur is a trusted advisor who informs their patients, all the while respecting the patients' rights to self-determination.

Another myth is that most lawsuits are frivolous. In fact, most have some basis in a real or perceived loss for the patient or the patient's family. Granted, the magnitude of some of the financial awards doled out in successful malpractice suits can be out of proportion to the loss, but that does not mean the patient had no reasonable basis for legal action. Malpractice suits and complaints damage your practice. Best practices demand that no patient concern be treated as trite or frivolous.

The prudent Healthcare Entrepreneur can take some other reasonable steps to minimize the likelihood of a patient lawsuit or complaint and mediate the damage when a complaint is filed. The first and perhaps most important step is to maintain a positive, compassionate, professional relationship with your patients — *all* your patients. The patient with whom you find it most difficult to form a bond may be the patient most likely to take action against you.

Communication is another valuable risk management tool. It is easy in the course of a busy day to get so focused on the core tasks associated with a patient contact that you forget to make a meaningful connection with the patient. Giving the patient the opportunity to tell you a bit about their life beyond what is ailing them can go a long way in the right direction.

Consider what an encounter might feel like from the patient's perspective when the patient has an opportunity to tell you a bit about their child's latest achievement or express a concern about how whatever is ailing them might affect their job, marriage, or longevity. True, the extra time you spend listening is time you could spend providing another billable service, but what good is that extra revenue if it is lost to defending and paying out a settlement in a lawsuit?

Documentation is another important tool in risk management. Documentation starts with informed consent and, in broad terms, means communicating to the patient what they will be experiencing, why, and with what risks. Informed consent includes apprising the patient of business practices the patient will be obliged to follow, as well as providing information about clinical procedures and their alternatives.

Providing informed consent can be a challenge because patients have different tolerances and needs for knowledge regarding their own healthcare. Nonetheless, from a liability management perspective, it is best to provide your patients with detailed information so they can assess their options and be truly well informed.

Written information should be provided in basic terms. Although there are no hard and fast rules about this, there are good reasons to provide written informed consent documents at a level a 12-year-old could understand. Videos in which the treating professional or a colleague explains a procedure can be a helpful adjunct in this regard. Because no written form will address every question every patient might have, it is important to ask each patient if they have any questions about what they have seen, heard, or read.

Another aspect of documentation involves charting. A patient's recollection of the "facts" will invariably differ from the recollection of the treating professional. As a rule, the longer the elapsed time between a procedure and the need to recall the procedure, the greater the distortion in everyone's memories. Chart notes should record each interaction with the patient in enough detail to keep the memories accurate. Ambiguity is the enemy. Where there is ambiguity, patients, juries, and disciplinary action boards will fill in the blanks with assumptions that best fit their own biases.

CHECKLIST 4

Elements of Informed Consent

Laws defining informed consent vary from jurisdiction to jurisdiction.

Standards by which the sufficiency of the information provided in an informed consent range from completely subjective to reasonable patient standards to reasonable doctor's standards. Each should be borne in mind.

Merely having a patient sign a consent form does not suffice. The "informed" part of the consent requires discussion, time to think and seek consultation, and opportunities to ask questions.

Among the elements that should be included in any informed consent are:

✓ The nature of the decision facing the patient.
✓ The specifics of what will occur in the procedure.
✓ Reasonable alternatives to the proposed procedure.
✓ The relevant risks, benefits, and uncertainties related to each of the patient's options.
✓ Documentation of the patient's understanding of what they have been told.
✓ The competent patient's signature endorsing the choice they make.

Professionals who find themselves relying almost exclusively on the preformatted charting language in their electronic records are likely leaving important information out of their chart notes and reports. Of course, chart notes should include all the elements needed to comply with legal and regulatory requirements and all those needed to show that the procedure met the requirements set by third-party payers for a payable service. In addition, all of the Healthcare Entrepreneur's actions and the patient's responses should also be recorded.

Many licensing complaints and medical malpractice claims arise from an omission, such as not warning a patient of known risks or missing a diagnosis. Only a proportion of malpractice claims are tied to an active professional error, such as performing the wrong procedure. Checklists and required fields in electronic chart notes can help minimize omissions.

ADDRESSING COMPLAINTS AND MALPRACTICE CLAIMS

Unfortunately, many competent professionals find themselves accused of malpractice at some point in their careers. When this occurs, it is important to manage the accusation carefully and appropriately. This means, among other things, avoiding the temptation to minimize the complaint because you see it as unfounded or because you believe that the patient values the relationship with you too much to truly pursue action against you.

Upon learning of a malpractice suit, the first step is to call an Attorney who is knowledgeable and experienced in this area of law. Your malpractice insurance policy probably requires you to also notify the insurance company of any possible claim. Have your Attorney handle everything on your behalf. Although some data support arguments in the opposite direction, the conventional wisdom is to avoid direct contact with the complainant unless advised to do otherwise by your Attorney. Let your Attorney be your guide and your mouthpiece.

Malpractice claims and other complaints can be distressing. The temptation to discuss the matter with friends and colleagues can be strong, especially if the case drags on interminably. Discussing the case with anyone but your Attorney and experts approved by the Attorney is an error.

Medical records, including billing records and any other documents related to an active or pending complaint or lawsuit, should be stored in a safe place. It is essential that no changes be made in the records. Now is not the time to flesh out the note that was a bit too sketchy when you originally wrote it.

Monitor yourself and your self-care. The emotional strain of being assaulted with a lawsuit or regulatory complaint can be intense. Keep an eye out for ways that the strain leaks through into your relationships with family, friends, employees, and patients. In a related vein, consider ways to manage and mediate the stress and strain. Redouble your self-care strategies to counterbalance the additional pressures.

TERMINATING PATIENT CARE

There are times when a professional might choose to withdraw from treating a patient. To avoid charges of patient abandonment, the Healthcare Entrepreneur must exit carefully, ethically, and in a legally appropriate fashion. At a minimum, the patient should be notified that they are being administratively discharged and, in general form, the reasons for the discharge. This can be done by certified letter with a receipt to be signed by the recipient and returned to the sender to verify that the notification was received. The letter should include the recommendation that care be continued with another professional, along with a list of other viable professionals to whom the patient can turn. A copy of the letter, the list, and the returned receipt should be placed in the patient's medical record, along with an objective summary of the reason(s) for terminating care. Professionals should offer to provide urgent and emergency care for a reasonable but finite amount of time until the patient can establish a relationship with another professional.

Labor Relations

P erhaps because there are only so many hours in a day or perhaps because four hands can accomplish twice as much as two hands, as a Healthcare Entrepreneur, you are likely to hire employees, supervise contractors, and perhaps take on partners. Having good relationships with co-workers is essential to maintaining a pleasant atmosphere in the office and adds to the positive ambiance. Good relations begin with the first encounter and continue until the co-worker leaves or retires, and perhaps beyond.

HIRING AND RETAINING VALUABLE EMPLOYEES

Hiring begins before you even post or advertise an open position. The first step in hiring is to write an in-depth job description that includes as much detail as possible about the tasks, functions, and responsibilities that go with the position (see Checklist 5).

Next, create a budget for the position. It makes no sense to pay an employee unless that employee is performing a function that is profitable or, at the very least, more cost-efficient than doing it yourself. To calculate the budget, simply estimate the amount of time the employee will be engaged in the various tasks associated with the job. By applying the proportion of time spent on a task, you can estimate the cost of performing the task. If the task generates revenue or saves another expense, that amount offsets the cost of the task.

When the cost of performing a task is higher than the amount of revenue generated or saved, as a savvy Healthcare Entrepreneur, you should think twice before proceeding. Is that task really necessary? What would you lose if you did without that job function? Is there a more cost-efficient way to achieve the goal?

CHECKLIST 5

Elements of a Job Description

✓ Title of position:
✓ About the company:
✓ Reports to:
✓ Department:
✓ Primary mission of the position:
✓ Summary of position:
✓ Duties, tasks, and responsibilities:
✓ Physical demands:
✓ Supervisory Responsibilities:
✓ Evaluations Metrics:
✓ Education and Experience:
✓ Required Skills/Abilities:
✓ Salary/wages:
✓ Benefits package:

Where and how you post or advertise an open position significantly influences the quality and type of applications you will receive, so choose your media carefully. A medium that works well for identifying office staff may be of little or no value when it comes to finding applicants for a professional position.

Some advertising media are costly, while others are free or nearly so. One option that tends to work well regardless of the available position is to use your existing contacts to spread the word that you have a position open. Listservs, your own contact lists, and word of mouth spread by current staff members are all available as free or very inexpensive ways to create interest in an open position. Local high schools, colleges, technical schools, and professional training programs are the funnels through which younger applicants file. Previously cultivated relations with guidance counselors and placement counselors in these institutions can be fruitful when it comes time to identify candidates for various support positions.

Most of the major professional societies have job boards and other media on which professional positions can be posted. Some of these are targeted to a specific profession; others tie into bigger networks, which can result in inappropriate applications from unqualified applicants. The same can be said for the commercial websites that advertise for all sorts of positions: on the one hand, many of these sites have a broad reach and on the other hand, they tend to garner applications that do not meet your requirements even if you use the screening questions that most sites provide. The result is extra cost per click expenses as well as the costs of culling the applications.

Employment agencies and professional recruiting companies, referred to as "head hunters," are available to help the time-strapped Healthcare Entrepreneur fill professional positions. These tend to be pricey; fee structures range from a flat fee to be paid as soon as a candidate is hired (i.e., before that candidate has brought in any revenues to offset the fee) to fees that are based on a percentage of the new employee's salary.

The larger recruiting companies tend to maintain rosters of applicants, which can give them a head start when it comes to filling a newly listed position. Other companies go to work finding candidates only after they have a contract to do so. Interview the specific recruiter who will be working with you before you retain them and find out how successful they have been filling similar positions in the past.

You will want to review each applicant's resume to make sure they have the needed education, training, and experience for a job. The resume or curriculum vita also tells you something about each candidate's work style, reliability, and personality. For example, typing errors in a resume suggests a subpar level of attention to detail. The candidate who describes their past positions in terms of the tasks they performed is different from the candidate who focuses on their accomplishments in previous jobs.

Contacting references, service club leaders, and others in the community is a step you should not skip. Even newcomers to the workforce should be able to provide professional references from teachers.

Once you have culled the applications and identified those applicants who appear to be viable, arrange for face-to-face interviews. If the applicant lives out of the area, consider video conferencing as an effective alternative. Interviews should be scheduled as soon as a candidate is identified as being of interest. Yours is probably not the only business to which each applicant has applied, so act promptly.

Effective interviews require pre-written lists of questions that you want answered along with an idea about the answers you hope to hear. It is also helpful to develop a list of questions you would expect an applicant to ask and a list of the traits and qualities you hope to see during the interview. The time and effort spent thinking about and developing these lists is time well spent. Without such lists, your interview may be heavily influenced by subjective impressions such as likeability and physical attractiveness. Successful interviewers consider the facts and then consider the subjective factors secondarily.

The conventional wisdom that you learn more by listening certainly holds true in interviewing. Give the applicant plenty of time to tell you about themselves and to ask questions. In fact, let them go first. When it is time for you to ask questions, make sure your questions are as open-ended as possible. Consider the difference between these two questions: "What are your weak suits?" versus "Tell me about a time you really messed up and what you did about it."

Present job offers in writing or, if made verbally, follow up with a written offer immediately thereafter. When offering an applicant a job, clearly state what the job entails, the salary being offered, the benefits associated with the position, and any other factors that might be significant. Request that the applicant accepts the job by returning a signed copy of the offer acknowledging the acceptance of the offer and the terms. This reduces the chance of misunderstandings and potential conflicts.

In most fields, the law of supply and demand governs the wages paid to the majority of employees. In the field of healthcare, however, other forces often are more influential than supply and demand. Several economic forces cause healthcare fees to remain flat over time when compared to the rise in fees and charges in other industries. This can limit your ability to pay attractive employees higher wages, even when the labor market is favorable to the job seeker.

Further complicating matters are myriad statutes and regulations that control how financial incentives can and cannot be used to attract healthcare professionals. So, although supply and demand certainly are factors when it comes to hiring workers, there are other factors that you must also take into account.

From a regulatory compliance perspective, the safest way to remunerate a healthcare employee is by a straight wage or salary that is guaranteed regardless of productivity. This eliminates any real or perceived room for concern about financial motives influencing clinical decision making. On the other side of the coin, flat salaries promote minimal performance; there is no financial incentive for the professional earning a flat salary to work overtime or take an emergency phone call in the middle of the night.

One solution to this dilemma is to add what is known as "additional compensation" for services above and beyond the typical call of duty. For example, if a professional has an annual salary of $104,000, the hourly wage is $50 per normal working hour. For time spent on call or responding to an emergency, the wage may be increased to time and a half, or $75.00 ($50.00 × 1.5) per hour paid as additional compensation.

An employed healthcare professional who is guaranteed a salary based on the fee structure at the time the professional signed the contract is insulated from getting a lesser salary if fee schedules decline in the future. The employer, on the other hand, will have less income, and perhaps even a loss, if their fee schedules are reduced. Contracts involving guaranteed payments should have clauses that permit changes and create elbow room in the event of untenable circumstances such as fee schedule reductions, claims rejected due to any act or omission by the employee, or natural disaster that chokes off revenues.

For similar reasons, giving raises can also be a problem in healthcare. Many businesses in other sectors have rules and procedures that help determine who gets raises and in what amount. Three common factors in determining raises include (1) the employee's recent performance, (2) the rate of inflation, and (3) the company's current profit margin. For example, a high-performing employee, living in a town where the inflation rate is, for the sake of discussion, 2.5%, working in a company that has made more profit than it had initially predicted, might get a raise of 5% based on the formula rate of inflation × 2. Another employee in the same circumstances whose job performance is acceptable but lackluster might get a lesser raise of 2.5% based on the formula of rate of inflation × 1. In both examples, rewarding the employee increases the likelihood of retaining that employee and encourages the employee to keep up the good work.

These formulas become financially unfeasible if revenues do not rise in proportion. Fortunately, there are options by which employees can be given needed raises without cutting into profits. For example, many support positions do not typically carry with them the responsibility for generating revenues even though, with a little bit of tweaking, they could do so. Consider a Receptionist who simply notes cancellations in the scheduling program. If that same Receptionist were trained to call patients who have not been seen for a while or have missed a recommended follow-up to fill the canceled appointment time, they would be generating revenues that can be used to fund raises.

Determining Salaries and Wages

Determining how much to pay employees requires some research, some calculations, and a bit of flexibility. The goal is to pay wages and salaries that your practice can afford and substantial enough to attract and retain the employees you need to run your business. Many factors go into determining a "fair wage."

Begin the process of setting wages by budgeting the position. When a job is income-generating, the range of possible wages for that position is bracketed between the net income generated and the legally mandated minimum wage. When a job does not directly generate revenue but is essential for functioning, the range of possible wages is much narrower. Some positions do not generate revenue directly but result in cost-savings that should be considered when budgeting the position. The budget should include the amount of revenue generated and the savings the position might create on the revenue side.

On the cost side of the budget, the amount of pay necessary to compete for talent is not the only variable. Don't forget to add in payroll taxes, benefits, dues, and training costs. Remember, a wage that was perfectly reasonable and viable when the local unemployment rate was high may not be sufficient to attract or retain employees when the unemployment rate drops.

Data regarding how much people in similar positions are being paid are readily available on the internet. Several commercial sites track and report wages by job title, geography, and even by company in some cases. There also are a number of government sites that are rife with such information. The federal Bureau of Labor Statistics (BLS) publishes searchable databases (www.bls.gov/data/#wages) along with guidance pertaining to benefits and other factors employers consider when filling an open position. Most states have their own Bureau of Labor Statistics or similar agency with a different name.

An often-overlooked resource is information about the amount government agencies pay employees with skills and training similar to what you are looking for. Sometimes, government positions have higher pay and more benefits than healthcare practices can afford. Job seekers and job hoppers will be attracted to higher wages. If you cannot match the competing compensation package, detail what it is about your practice that makes accepting a lower wage worthwhile and seek out candidates who value what you offer.

You can learn a lot about the range of wages being offered for a given position in your community by perusing classified ads. Remember to take into account the differences between the position you are offering and similar positions that are being advertised by others; these variations may account for substantial differences in wages offered.

For example, an ad for a Registered Nurse might offer considerably more remuneration than you imagined the position would require. However, even if the job title is the same, there are significant differences between nursing in a medical office during regular business hours and nursing in a skilled nursing facility on the night shift. The latter position is harder to fill and will require higher pay to attract applicants.

Employing Other Professionals

Business owners often proclaim that personnel management is among the toughest parts of their job. Hiring and managing professional colleagues can be a particular challenge, as it requires skills and insights beyond those needed to hire and manage the support staff.

For example, it is important to understand why different people choose particular work environments. Some licensed professionals prefer to print business cards, hang out a shingle, and go to work for themselves; others prefer to work for a hospital. Only a subset of professionals prefers to work in a group practice.

When evaluating a candidate, be sure that the candidate's aspirations and work style align with those of your business. Changes in staff, especially clinical staff, are expensive in terms of monetary costs and in terms of reputation and patient satisfaction. To minimize the risk of a short-tenured relationship, assess the "goodness-of-fit" before offering a candidate a job.

Another question to consider when evaluating a professional candidate is where else the candidate has applied. A prospective employee who has applied at many places, ranging from a large hospital to a small practice, is casting a wide net without regard for where they will be most satisfied. Maybe the person believes they will be happy in any environment, no matter the size. Or the applicant may not yet have figured out what kind of environment would suit them best. While there are certainly exceptions to the rule, either situation bodes poorly for long-term employment.

Some applicants are shopping around for the highest pay they can find. This, too, should send up warning signs. At a minimum, this strategy implies that the applicant is heavily influenced by extrinsic rewards— which may be fine as long as you are able and willing to keep meeting their extrinsic needs and desires. However, people who lean more heavily toward extrinsic reward systems tend to develop increasingly voracious appetites. Their need for rewards grows over time. Eventually, another employer may offer them a higher reward, and you will once again be in the position of having to fill a vacancy.

The same holds true at the opposite end of the spectrum. Some applicants make it clear that they are motivated by intrinsic factors and may struggle in a for-profit environment. Unfortunately, there is no perfect balance of intrinsic and extrinsic reward affinity in any given candidate. Arguably, the best person for your practice is one whose intrinsic–extrinsic balance is similar to yours.

For most people, completing advanced training in a profession requires some sense of independence and self-confidence. This does not mean that all professionals are independent or self-confident in every way; it simply means that when they take on the "mantle" of a professional, even as a student or resident, they can rise to the occasion as needed. To complicate matters, a person's sense of self-confidence or independence may vary, depending on the function being performed. The clinician who is quite confident in their ability to minister to patients independently may have trepidations about marketing or managing the business aspects of a practice.

Rather than automatically dismissing these candidates, discuss options such as training to expand the breadth of the candidate's confidence.

There is a long-standing debate among human resources professionals regarding whether it is best to hire people who are similar to the boss or people who have some complementary differences from the boss. One of the primary arguments favoring hiring those who differ is that they will bring to your organization a different perspective. Fresh eyes and new perspectives can help you expand your business. On the other side of the coin, the differences may result in occasional conflict. Avoiding the risks of discord by hiring in your own image means giving up opportunities to broaden your own perspective.

It can be tempting to ask professional applicants to submit to a battery of personnel screening tests as part of the selection process. Such evaluations can guide decisions about hiring and decisions about how that person will serve once hired. Such testing should always be outsourced by any Healthcare Entrepreneur who is not trained in and set up to provide it. The reason has less to do with ensuring the quality of the data garnered and more to do with avoiding liability. An array of fairly complex laws govern the use of such tests in employment circumstances. Companies that do not routinely provide such services are unlikely to have the policies, procedures, and structures in place that are necessary to avoid stepping into a legal minefield.

The Progressive Corrective Action Plan

Laws and standards pertaining to managing, disciplining, and terminating employees vary from state to state. Some states have complex and detailed labor laws; other so-called "right to work" states take a more hands-off approach to regulating the relationship between employers and employees. Regardless of the legal responsibilities you have as an employer, common sense and financial efficiency dictate that you make every reasonable effort to help your employees do well on the job. Replacing employees is expensive.

One tool to help employees succeed is the Progressive Corrective Action Plan (PCAP). PCAPs emphasize professional growth and improved performance. When you approach employees with these emphases in mind, they are more likely to buy-in and less likely to take a defensive posture. You can use the document and the associated discussions to build your relationship with the employee whose performance is being addressed. This approach stands in contrast to the Disciplinary Action Plan (DAP), which is brought into play when an employee is unable or unwilling to make necessary changes. Both the PCAP and DAP serve to document the fact that you have taken all reasonable steps before the unsuccessful employee is terminated.

A basic approach to performance improvement has three phases: (1) verbal warnings, (2) the written PCAP, and, if necessary, (3) termination of employment. Verbal warnings should be communicated to the employee privately and discussions should be well documented. Documentation should be retained in the employee's personnel file. This is an opportunity to coach the employee; it also is an opportunity to learn from the employee's perspective what, if anything, should be revised in their job description and the practice's policies and procedures.

A written PCAP is the final attempt to resolve problems that have not yet been satisfactorily resolved. The shift into this phase puts the employee on written notice that their job is at risk. When you draft a PCAP, be as specific as possible about perceived infractions and problems, expected outcomes, steps to be taken to achieve those outcomes, and a time frame during which the employee must reach the stated goal(s). The PCAP also lets the employee know what steps you, as their employer, are and are not willing to take to help them succeed. For example, relieving an employee of one task may resolve a problem.

Employees sign the PCAP to indicate that they read and understood what was written. When an employee refuses to sign the written warning, the refusal should be noted on the warning. Employees should have the opportunity to respond in writing to the PCAP as well.

When an employee's performance falls below your reasonable expectations, you should take prompt and appropriate actions because problems seldom resolve with time. In fact, they are more likely to become worse. Employee underperformance typically has several negative effects. One effect is the employee's negative influence on other employees, including a general lowering of the bar for everyone else's performance. Working with underperforming co-workers can lead to burnout by employees who are covering for the problems created by the underperformer.

Other common circumstances that warrant prompt attention include excessive absences or frequent tardiness by otherwise-desirable employees. Employees should be required to begin active, productive work at the scheduled start of their day. Employees who are permitted to arrive as their shift begins and walk out of the door at the end are wasting valuable work time getting computers and other equipment warmed up and shut down. Even when these behaviors are tolerable to the employer, they can have a corrosive effect on other employees and, therefore, should be addressed.

> **TIP:** Computer login and logout times can be used to track tardiness and under-performance for many positions.

Insubordination is another concern that is too corrosive to ignore. Healthcare Entrepreneurs value open, honest input and feedback from their employees;

however, the employees must provide their input in a respectful manner that does not undermine the authority and credibility of those in leadership positions, be they owners or managers. Insubordinate employees are more likely than most to be acting inappropriately with other people as well, including patients. Consequently, no incidence of insubordination should go unaddressed. Responses should include documentation of the offense and plans for remediation, including training in assertive communication.

When it comes to motivating employees to improve performance, carefully chosen words are particularly important from a liability perspective. Consider the difference between "Employee lied by stating that 'I was in a car wreck'" versus "A subsequent check of the motor vehicle accident reports on file with the highway patrol failed to confirm the employee's report of a motor vehicle accident. Nor did the employee provide requested documentation to substantiate the statement." At the bottom line, stick to the facts. Avoid opinions, judgments, inferences, and summary conclusions.

Even when everyone involved is doing their best, sometimes employment should be terminated. Involuntary terminations should be handled with as much attention to detail and procedure as possible. You or a manager should go through a series of previously drafted steps to ensure that the termination is clear and clean, with no room for further action. Termination interviews are two-sided conversations in which employees should be advised about what earned pay and pay for unused vacation time is due to them, their access to health insurance, the need to return all company property, and other information. Changing locks and passwords and obtaining a forwarding address for the employee are important as well.

An employee's service should be ended immediately in some cases, such as theft, violence, and maltreatment of patients or co-workers. Immediate means *immediate.* Too often, to avoid the inconvenience and tumult that arises when a key employee leaves suddenly, employers "allow" employees who know they have been or will be "fired" to keep working for some period of time. Although it is sometimes possible for this to work out, more often it is a recipe for problems, sometimes of disastrous proportions.

HIRING INDEPENDENT CONTRACTORS

Employers may be tempted to classify those who perform work for them as independent contractors in hopes of avoiding the expenses of taxes or benefits. Agencies such as the Internal Revenue Service (IRS) issue criteria that must be met in order to classify an employee as an independent contractor. Regardless of their job classification, you must treat workers who meet the criteria of employee as such. For example, you must withhold income taxes and pay Social Security, Medicare taxes, and unemployment tax on wages paid to the employee. You are also responsible for matching the employee's contribution to Social Security and Medicare.

Because hiring an employee can be more expensive than retaining a contractor, it may be tempting to designate as many people as possible as contractors. However, doing so inappropriately can place the company in a bad position with the IRS. What's more, miscategorized personnel can bring legal actions to recover the money they lost due to being miscategorized.

The IRS considers three sets of criteria in classifying a worker. One criterion is how much control the employer has over the worker's behavior. In general, when the person performing a job controls what they do and how they do it, they may qualify as a contractor. For example, if you retain a Web Designer who has free rein to achieve your stated goals using the way they think is best, they may be regarded as a contractor. On the other hand, if you are evaluating the Web Designer's performance throughout the development phase, they may be more likely to be considered an employee because you are exercising behavioral control.

Another criterion involves financial considerations and whether the worker is free to work for others. A Certified Registered Nurse Anesthetist (CRNA) who works at several surgery centers on an as-needed basis might be regarded as a contractor. However, if one of the surgery centers reimburses the CRNA for liability insurance or continuing education expenses, doing so would be more in line with the definition of employee.

Finally, the relationship between a worker and an employer must be considered. In healthcare settings, this relationship is often detailed in a contract and is defined by factors such as whether benefits or paid time off are provided. Simply labeling a contract as an "Employment Agreement" or "Contractor's Agreement" does not automatically place the worker in one of those two categories. See Checklist 6 for an outline of IRS considerations in classifying workers.

Employers who retain contractors must obtain a completed IRS Form W9 from each prior to the commencement of work. At the end of each tax year, the employer reports how much was paid to the contractor using IRS Form 1099 and sends copies of this form to the contractor and to the IRS accompanied by IRS Form 1096. Because the business does not withhold money from wages paid to contractors, the contractors themselves are responsible for paying the requisite taxes and withholdings.

When working with contractors, it's critical to take several additional steps beyond those you might take when considering a new employee. First, always complete a thorough background check. At a minimum, check references and confirm

CHECKLIST 6

Employee or Contractor?
IRS Considerations

Behavioral control considerations:

✓ How much training does the employer provide?

✓ How detailed are the employer's instructions?

✓ Will the worker be evaluated based on actions or outcomes?

Financial control considerations:

✓ Who owns the equipment needed to do the job?

✓ Will the worker be reimbursed for expenses?

✓ Is remuneration fixed, or can it vary?

✓ Is the worker free to perform work for others?

Relationship considerations

✓ Is there a written contract between the employer and the worker?

✓ Does the worker receive or is the worker eligible for benefits?

✓ How permanent is the relationship expected to be?

✓ How essential to the business are the worker's functions?

appropriate licensing. For many contracted positions, such as billing services, it is a good idea to consider bonding the contractor. For example, even if you are confident that the billing service you use is staffed by honest people, honest people sometimes change when their life circumstances change. Bonding the contracted employee or the billing service may mitigate difficulties if the contractor misbehaves. When a worker has been bonded, an insurance policy has been taken out on that person for the amount of the bond, which is usually a large sum of money, insulating your business from harm at the hands of contractors or others.

Any contractor who routinely or may incidentally encounter Protected Health Information must read, sign, and agree to comply with the practice's HIPAA compliance policies. It is not sufficient to rely on verbal agreements. Contractors must sign a HIPAA-compliant Business Associates Agreement (BAA). Sample language for Business Associates Agreements is posted by the Centers for Medicare & Medicaid Services (CMS) at www.hhs.gov/hipaa/for-professionals/covered-entities/sample-business-associate-agreement-provisions/index.html. Because the language changes from time to time, forms such as this should be reviewed at least annually to ensure they are fully compliant.

OUTSOURCING WORK

Operating a healthcare practice requires more skills and knowledge than any one person, including the owner, can reasonably bring to the table. When a set of skills or a body of knowledge is needed on a routine basis, the practice should hire an employee to provide the skills or knowledge. Sometimes, skills or knowledge are needed only on a part-time or occasional basis, or there are office space limitations, or other factors make it unreasonable to hire an employee. In these circumstances, Healthcare Entrepreneurs outsource the work.

Outsourcing entails contracting with an independent person or company to do work the practice needs to have done. Examples of outsourcing include retaining a cleaning service to clean the office or retaining a CPA or Attorney to file taxes or write contracts. In healthcare, billing and collections functions are often outsourced.

One common justification for outsourcing is the lack of time to supervise a new employee. This usually is not a good reason to outsource. The person or company hired to do the outsourced work will need supervision, just as an in-house employee would. Even if saving time is the motivation for outsourcing, it is important to schedule time to supervise the firm or person retained to do the job.

Determining whether to outsource and whom to retain requires some thought and calculations. Three factors should be considered.

1. Consider the cost of the outsourcing options. You can do this by requesting bids from vetted vendors.
2. Consider what would be gained from outsourcing. A company or person who cannot or will not provide you with data on past performance should not be considered.
3. Weigh these calculations against the cost-benefit ratio of performing the needed function in-house.

DISCLOSURE

The author of this book is a Consultant specializing in the business of healthcare practice. In the service of full disclosure, any biases reflected in this section are both intentional and borne of decades of experience.

Hiring Consultants

Consultants are people who have knowledge of *and* experience in some area. Consultants bring fresh eyes, new perspectives, and a library of lessons learned by watching the successes and failures of their other clients. This makes competent Consultants invaluable resources who can help identify and launch new opportunities, recognize the strengths and weaknesses of your practice, and manage certain projects that would otherwise distract from your main business.

For these reasons and more, Consultants often help Healthcare Entrepreneurs earn or save considerably more than the Consultant's fees cost.

When selecting a Consultant, it is important to ensure their knowledge and experience are relevant to the goals you have for them. For example, a Consultant who has a proven track record of building a successful solo practice may have some, but not all, of the knowledge and experience needed to help you develop a successful group practice.

Before interviewing a prospective Consultant, list the skills and experiences you think they will need to get your job done. Then question them about their skills and experiences to determine if there is a match.

> **TIP:** Professional Consultants read management journals, attend healthcare management conventions, and track important events such as the passage of new laws on an on-going basis. Before retaining a Consultant, ask them what they do to keep abreast of the industry.

Too often, businesses wait until they are faced with a clear problem before turning to a Consultant for assistance. Savvy Healthcare Entrepreneurs routinely call in Consultants to keep their business dynamic, growing, on track, and out of trouble. Consider the difference between the practice owner who brings in a Consultant to iron out problems in the billing office versus the Healthcare Entrepreneur who hires a Consultant to review or develop the operating procedures for the billing department. Consider, too, the owner who, in hopes of sparing the expense, waits a few years to hire a Consultant and finds that revenues have been lost that could have been captured all along.

The fees Consultants charge are an investment in your business. To get your money's worth, be prepared to implement most, if not all, of the Consultant's recommendations. If you have concerns about a particular recommendation, don't just toss the recommendation aside. Instead, discuss your concerns with the Consultant and together you may be able to revise the recommendation so it has value for your business. See Checklist 7 for a list of Consultants you should have on hand.

WHEN EMPLOYEES LEAVE OR RETIRE

Sometimes employees remain with a practice for a short period of time after they have announced their intention to leave. For example, a support staff member

---

CHECKLIST 7

Consultants You Should Have on Hand

Just as it is best for patients to have a relationship with their physician before there is a medical crisis, it is best for businesses to have relationships with key consultants before they are in dire need of that consultant's services. Consultants, like healthcare professionals in clinical practice, are more likely to make room in their schedule for a client with whom they have worked in the past, even if that work is limited to a brief getting to know each other meeting. These Consultants are valuable to your practice:

✓ CPA

✓ Attorney

✓ Information technology consultant

✓ Marketing and public relations consultant

✓ Practice management consultant

✓ Payroll and personnel management consultant

✓ Investment advisor

---

provides two weeks' notice of their intent to terminate their employment. In such cases, employees enter an unfamiliar twilight zone — no matter how hard they try to maintain a normal routine, the days leading up to a planned exit are different and deserve to be treated accordingly. Employees who are scheduled to leave their jobs should be monitored for changes in productivity, demeanor, and behavior.

Some employers react negatively when an employee announces their intention to leave. Some go so far as to send people home immediately when they give their two weeks' notice. Some simply cut back on opportunities for the departing employee. Usually, such responses are counterproductive and send the message to others that they should keep their plans to themselves and notify their employer at the last possible moment. These reactions also taint the relationship between the organization and the person who is leaving. Remember, today's employee may be tomorrow's referral source or the gatekeeper to a desirable opportunity.

A WORD ABOUT CONTRACTS AND TRUST

Business owners typically spend several hours a day at their place of business, and they depend on co-owners and employees to promote their prosperity. For these reasons and others, it is important to be as certain as you can be that any newcomer to the business, be it an employee or a future partner, is someone you believe you can trust. If you are not sure you can trust someone, it is wise not to let them in the door.

Trust among co-workers is similar to the trust between a wife and husband. Trust, in its essence, is the confidence that two people have that both will diligently avoid doing anything that would be harmful to the other. We like to say that we trust our partners implicitly, across the board; however, even trustworthy people acting in good faith can behave in ways that may be harmful to our interests. That's why it is essential that contracts be drawn. The relationship itself should be formed on a baseline of trust; the trust will be built and maintained through a written contract.

A well-written contract includes more than just the legally necessary clauses and language. To guide your Attorney in drafting such a contract, take a thorough inventory of everything you anticipate might arise as a point of contention. The contract should be your guide as to how these problems will be managed should they arise. Often, this can be accomplished with global language, such as a mandate that employees shall abide by the policies and procedures of the business.

Working With Insurance Companies

Although insurance has been around for a long time, insurance to hedge against the costs of receiving healthcare services was not introduced in the United States until the middle of the 19th century. Since then, the insurance industry has grown and morphed into the behemoth it is today. The majority of Americans now rely on some form of health insurance to hedge against healthcare expenses, purchasing it from private insurance companies or through government programs such as Medicare and Medicaid.

INSURANCE COMPANY RELATIONSHIPS

Some Healthcare Entrepreneurs refuse to work with insurance companies, citing the administrative burden and diminished profits associated with accepting a patient's insurance as their source of payment. Health insurance has become so ubiquitous, however, that most Healthcare Entrepreneurs do form relationships with and work with insurance companies.

In the future, more and more healthcare professionals likely will work directly for insurance companies and related entities such as Health Maintenance Organizations (HMOs) and clinics. For the time being, most healthcare professionals work with, not for, insurance companies.

From the insurance industry's perspective, your interactions with the insurers are voluntary collaborations in the service of the patient; no employment relationship is created. Nonetheless, the insurance industry wields tremendous influence over the clinical and business practices of most healthcare professionals.

Even if you choose not to accept insurance, you should be familiar with the insurance industry and the laws surrounding it. Laws on the books in several jurisdictions protect insured patients from paying out of pocket even when they voluntarily choose to do so. For example, in some jurisdictions, it is illegal to charge a patient insured by an HMO for services for which the HMO would have paid if the patient had chosen to receive services from an HMO-approved source. Another example is the prohibition against collecting copayments from patients who have a secondary insurance policy through Medicaid, even when the Healthcare Entrepreneur does not accept Medicaid.

When you provide services to an uninsured patient, the relationship is straightforward. In that circumstance, two people choose to work together because one desires, and is willing to pay for, the services of the other. When insurance is involved, the relationships become much more complicated. The relationship of the patient to the Healthcare Entrepreneur, the relationship of the patient to the insurer, and the relationship of the Healthcare Entrepreneur to the insurance company all must be considered.

The wisdom of "two's company, three's a crowd" can ring true when the insurer becomes a third entity in the patient–Healthcare Entrepreneur relationship. There is plenty of room for triangulation when one of the three players takes advantage of their relationship with another player to influence the third player. An example is when an insurance company tells an insured patient that the patient's claim was rejected because the billing professional used the "wrong" diagnosis. In this context, the term "wrong" does not mean "incorrect." It means the accurate diagnosis is not covered under that patient's insurance policy. Nonetheless, the professional's credibility is compromised, along with the quality of the professional's relationship with the patient.

Therefore, it is essential to be as specific as possible when requesting insurance companies' precertification and preapproval of services. A single variable might change a covered procedure to a noncovered procedure. For example, most insurance policies cover marriage counseling as a mental health service and are quick to tell their customers that this is the case. In actuality, the coverage often applies only if the insured person needs treatment for a specific illness, such as schizophrenia, that is covered (i.e., not excluded) by the policy. When, as is most often the case, an insured person seeks marriage counseling to address strife in a marriage, the claim is usually rejected as not being medically necessary. The Marriage Counselor is left holding the bag if they had previously agreed to accept the patient's insurance as the source of payment. Often, the Marriage Counselor cannot back-bill the patient for the rejected claim.

GLOSSARY OF HEALTH INSURANCE TERMS

The insurance industry has its own vocabulary and jargon; frequently, the meaning of terms in the insurance lexicon is very different from common usage. Healthcare Entrepreneurs need to understand the jargon; failure to do so can negatively impact billings, collections, contract negotiations, and other essential functions.

Allowed Amount

An allowed amount is the maximum amount the insurance company or other payer will pay for a given item or service. The maximum amount may be determined by regulations, by fiat, or by negotiations between the Healthcare Entrepreneur and the payer. Actual free market forces have little influence in determining allowed amounts. The terms of your agreement with the payer determine whether you can collect from the patient the difference between the allowed amount and your actual fee.

Appeals

The rejection or underpayment of an insurance claim does not have to be the end of the story. You can file written appeals with payers to request a more thorough consideration of a claim that you believe was misprocessed. Appeals should cite the reasons that reconsideration is warranted and what the expected outcome should be. The appeal must make it clear that all the insurance company's medical necessity criteria are met, or that a specific criterion is particularly unreasonable in a given patient's case. Typically, the insurance company dictates procedures that must be followed before the appeal will be considered.

Assignment

Insurance policies involve contracts between patients and insurance companies. Accordingly, benefit payments from the insurer should go to the insured. However, patients can "assign" the benefits due to them from a third-party payer to the Healthcare Entrepreneur who renders services. Assignment allows the insurer to pay the Healthcare Entrepreneur directly. Accepting the assignment of benefits often is contingent on terms with which the Healthcare Entrepreneur may not be comfortable. For example, accepting assignment often means that the Healthcare Entrepreneur agrees to be paid no more than the insurance company's allowed amount. There is no option to bill the patient for the remainder of the fee. The unpaid portion of the bill, if any, must be written off.

Balance Billing

When the allowed amount paid for a claim is less than the amount billed, the resulting balance due, in some circumstances, can be billed to the patient. This is known as balance billing or back-billing. Many contracts between professionals and payers prohibit or restrict balance billing. It is important to know which patients can and cannot be held responsible for the portion of a bill that is not covered by insurance.

Burden of Enrollment

Like any business, insurance companies can improve their profit margins by trimming minor costs. As a result, there is a trend in the industry to shift responsibilities for functions that serve only the insurance companies' interests. Time-consuming tasks such as applying for and renewing credentials on the insurance companies' panels of approved professionals are prime examples of expensive functions performed by professional practices that benefit only the insurance company. Collectively, these costs are referred to as the burden of enrollment.

Capitation

Capitation is one of the payment models used to tie service usage to Healthcare Entrepreneur income. In its basic form, the capitation model calls for Healthcare Entrepreneurs to be paid a predetermined amount of money to care for a specified number of patients in a specified time frame. If the cost of patient care exceeds the amount of money to be paid, the Healthcare Entrepreneur will sustain a genuine financial loss. On the other hand, if the Healthcare Entrepreneur limits the expenses associated with caring for the patients in the group, the Healthcare Entrepreneur can profit.

This model appeals to Healthcare Entrepreneurs who want to have more control of any cap on their income. In exchange, the Healthcare Entrepreneur accepts more financial risk. Capitated contracts should be carefully thought through in consultation with practice Consultants, actuarial professionals, and Attorneys.

Coinsurance

Insurance policies often require patients to pay some portion of each bill they receive; this can be accomplished through several mechanisms. One mechanism is coinsurance. Often expressed as percentage of the bill, coinsurance is one of the amounts the patient must pay for services received.

For example, if an insurance policy calls for 20% coinsurance, the patient must pay $20 to cover the proportion of a $100 charge that the insurance company will not pay. Related terms include deductible, copayment, and copay.

Coordination of Benefits

Sometimes more than one third-party payer is responsible for paying a patient's medical bill and there must be a coordination of benefits (COB). A typical example occurs when the patient has purchased secondary insurance to cover the deductibles, copayments, and coinsurance that the terms of their primary insurance calls for the patient to pay. Other common examples include cases in which worker's compensation or automobile insurance policies are used to pay for some portion of a bill. In such cases, the payment of the insurance "benefits" must be coordinated. Sometimes, but not always, the payers coordinate the payment of benefits.

> **TIP:** Some insurance policies require the patient to pay both a coinsurance amount and a copay amount at each visit. Do not forget to collect both when this is the case.

Typically, there is little for the Healthcare Entrepreneur to do other than to track the payments or submit billings to secondary payers. However, it is important to know whether insurers other than the patient's primary insurer will be involved in paying you. Use new patient intake forms to inquire whether the patient has a secondary insurance policy, has been injured on the job, or is seeking your services as a result of an automobile accident.

Copayment

Commonly referred to as "copay," this is the fee the patient pays to the professional for services rendered or goods sold. Typically, the copay is expressed as a specific dollar amount rather than as a percentage of a bill. In fact, many copay amounts are unrelated to the amount of the bill; rather, they are associated with a cost per visit. So, for example, one policy may have a $20 copay for an outpatient office visit; another may have the same copay unless the visit is to a specialist, in which case the copay is likely to be higher.

Deductible Amount

Many insurance policies leave the responsibility for paying most, or all, of medical bills to the patient until the bills reach a certain threshold known as the deductible. Bills in excess of the deductible amount are paid, at least in part, by the insurance company. The cost of purchasing a policy with a high deductible is lower than the cost of the same policy with a higher deductible, so many patients purchase policies with very high deductibles. If the deductible is high enough, many people will fail to reach the deductible amount each year and the insurance company's responsibility will be nil.

Because deductible amounts typically renew each year, it is essential to know how much of each patient's deductible has been paid before each visit. The insurance company will not pay claims filed on behalf of a patient who has not yet met the deductible. If the claim is rejected, the bill can be sent to the patient; however, such bills can be difficult to collect and too frequently become converted into bad debts. Using the insurance websites discussed in Chapter 2, the savvy Healthcare Entrepreneur can know in advance whether a patient has met their deductible. Knowing this allows the Healthcare Entrepreneur to collect accurate fees in advance, thus reducing billing costs and bad debt.

Because deductible amounts sometimes confuse even seasoned professionals, an example is in order. Consider a patient who holds a policy with a $3,000 deductible that renews at the beginning of each calendar year. Until the patient has paid $3,000 in fees out of pocket, the insurance company will not pay anything. The Healthcare Entrepreneur must collect all fees directly from the patient. When the same patient with the same policy has met and exceeded the deductible, the insurance company will begin to pay the bills. At that point, the practice can begin to bill the insurance company directly and expect payment. As soon as the calendar year changes, the deductible is reset and the burden to pay all new bills falls back to the patient.

Insurance policies sometimes set one deductible amount for services rendered by professionals who are in that insurance company's network of professionals and another for "out-of-network" professionals. By setting the out-of-network deductible at a level much higher than the deductible for in-network services, the insurance company penalizes patients for choosing a healthcare professional who will not accept the company's reduced fee schedules.

Another common variant of the deductible amount is the family deductible, as opposed to the individual deductible. A person who has met the individual deductible may have family members who have not. It behooves each practice to know in advance what each patient's deductible amounts are and to collect fees accordingly.

> **TIP:** As is often the case at the beginning of each year, many approved insurance claims must still be paid by the patient because their deductible amount has not been met. Consider collecting a deposit or fees up-front until there is evidence that the patient has met their deductible amount.

Diagnosis-Related Groups

Diagnosis-related groups (DRGs), originally developed to control inpatient costs, establish a fixed cost for treating various diagnoses and clusters of diagnoses. Hospitals and Healthcare Entrepreneurs are paid a predetermined amount based on the DRG under which a patient is admitted. This is known as a "prospective payment." When treatment costs exceed the amount paid for with the DRG, the service provider loses money. When treatment is provided for less than the DRG pays, the service provider enjoys a healthier profit margin for that case.

Predictably, the system has unearthed several problems, including the financial incentive to discharge patients prematurely. As is often the case in healthcare regulation, the "solution" comes in the form of more regulations, such as those that penalize hospitals for having to readmit patients soon after discharge.

Fee For Service

When the relationship between a patient and their treating Healthcare Entrepreneur is free of third-party payers, a Fee-For-Service (FFS) relationship is created. The Healthcare Entrepreneur and patient are free to choose mutually agreeable treatment plans and mutually agreeable fees. The patient is solely responsible for the cost of the care.

Many professionals limit their practices to fee-for-service relationships only. Some do so to keep their focus on clinical work rather than business functions; others do so knowing that it takes relatively few patients paying the full fee for services to generate as much profit as would be generated by a larger number of insured patients paying at a discounted rate.

In-Network and Out-of-Network

To fully appreciate the meaning of the term "network" in the health insurance context, it is necessary to keep the laws of supply and demand in mind. Healthcare reform has provided the insurance industry with control over both the supply of patients (i.e., the demand for services) and the supply of professionals available to serve those patients. The supply of patients is controlled by simply selling insurance policies. The pool of labor is controlled by creating networks of professionals and facilities that are willing to provide services at rates that are significantly discounted. Professionals in the network are known as in-network providers. All others are considered out-of-network providers.

> The term "providers" is used here because doing so is necessary to define a term. It is used sparingly throughout the rest of this book. The term "providers" is a derogatory, dehumanizing term that serves to limit the professionalism and special relationship with patients that doctors and other professionals have always enjoyed. The term instead connotes interchangeable "providers" of services with whom patients have a business relationship. Healthcare Entrepreneurs should avoid the term and object when it is used in their presence.

Modifiers

The codes used by most Healthcare Entrepreneurs to identify procedures they have performed come from the Current Procedural Terminology (CPT) manual, a copyrighted publication of the American Medical Association (AMA). These codes tend to be specific in their descriptions of what each coded procedure entails. When a specific procedure is performed in a manner that deviates from the code that best describes the procedure, modifiers can sometimes be appended to account for the deviation. For example, if a required element is intentionally omitted from a procedure, add the modifier -52 to indicate that the procedure performed involved less than the requisite array of elements.

Noncovered Services

Also known as exclusions, noncovered services are services, diagnoses, and products for which the insurance company will not pay, such as preventative services. Even common, frequently used services and oft-occurring diagnoses can be listed as noncovered services in a given policy. It is essential that you know what is and is not covered by each patient's policy. This information can be found using the websites discussed in Chapter 2 and the insurers medical necessity manuals.

Not Medically Necessary

Do not skip this definition even though you assume you know what the term means. As a healthcare professional, you have been taught how to assess the clinical value of the procedures and products you recommend to your patients. Interventions that are not needed to accomplish your patient's goal of wellness are generally recognized as not medically necessary.

This is not the definition that applies when the term "not medically necessary" is used in the context of health insurance. There, the term is used to label noncovered services, services that are not in sync with the insurance company's clinical protocols, and services that are not in line with the insurance company's provider manuals. Even a common diagnostic test that is routinely run to confirm a diagnosis can be declared not medically necessary if the insurance company decides that the diagnosis should be based solely on other criteria.

> **TIP:** Most insurers' provider manuals are available online and are worth checking with some frequency since they are subject to change.

Patients receive notifications from insurance companies informing them how a claim has been processed. When a claim is deemed not medically necessary, this term is used in the notice, leading the patient to doubt their healthcare professionals' conduct and judgment. Patient education is necessary to combat these misunderstandings.

Place of Service

Services that are routinely covered by an insurance policy when provided in a professional's outpatient office may not be covered when rendered in another environment, such as the patient's home. Sometimes, the services of a consulting Healthcare Entrepreneur in a hospital or Skilled Nursing Facility (SNF) are not covered because the service is bundled into a flat fee paid to the facility. Therefore, before rendering services outside of your office, it is essential to confirm that the intended place of service will not invalidate a claim.

Preauthorization

The terms "precertification" and "preauthorization" are often used interchangeably, yet they refer to different processes. Both are expensive, time-consuming processes that, at times, can take the better part of an hour. Failure to go through these steps will result in a rejected claim. Even when an authorizing code is obtained, the claim may still be rejected if the payer subsequently determines that some aspect of the service was not considered when the procedure was preauthorized. To obtain preauthorization, you must provide the insurer with a data set supporting the need for the treatment or other procedures you are contemplating. The insurer evaluates the data to determine whether there might be a different way to accomplish the stated goals. Remember, just because an insurer declines to preauthorize your treatment plan, that does not mean you should abandon the plan. It does mean that the patient must choose between paying for the recommended course of care personally or foregoing the treatment or procedure.

Precertification

Precertification is the process insurance companies and managed care organizations use to control the utilization of services. Healthcare Entrepreneurs planning to render services to an insured patient often must obtain precertification by contacting the insurance company and obtaining a code number authorizing the planned procedures. This usually can be accomplished online, by fax, or by telephone.

Relative Value Units

The Centers for Medicare & Medicaid Services (CMS) and others, relies on an ever-changing system by which Relative Value Units (RVUs) are assigned to procedures performed by healthcare professionals. RVUs are used to determine the value of each procedure and, ultimately, the fee that will be paid for that procedure.

Several factors go into the assignment of an RVU. First, the professional's time, skill, and training are assigned a value, known as the "Work RVU." Second, the costs of operating the type of facility that would render the service in question are estimated and calculated into an "Expense RVU". Another factor used in determining an RVU and typically given a small weight is based on the costs of professional liability insurance. Adjustments are then made for the costs of practicing in different geographic localities and the setting (inpatient or outpatient) in which the procedure will be rendered. Finally, a conversion factor is applied to derive a dollar value for each RVU.

Although few Healthcare Entrepreneurs will be called upon to calculate an RVU, it is worth having at least a passing familiarity with the formula because these calculations determine fees and payments. RVUs influence even non-Medicare payments because it is common in healthcare to negotiate private sector rates as a proportion of Medicare's rates. The formula is:

$$\text{Assigned Value of the Procedure (RVU)} =$$
$$(\text{Work RVU} + \text{Practice Expense RVU} + \text{Malpractice RVU}) \times \text{Conversion Factor}$$

Single-Case Agreements

There are times when an out-of-network professional may want to render services to a patient who is unable or unwilling to pay on a fee-for-service basis. An example is when a long-standing patient or a patient in the midst of ongoing treatment switches insurance companies. In these cases, it is sometimes possible to negotiate a one-time agreement with the patient's insurance carrier or managed care panel. Known as Single Case Agreements (SCAs), these agreements ensure that the insurance company will pay some or all the fees accrued in the case.

Typically, the insurance company will insist that the services be rendered at its reduced fee schedule. Healthcare Entrepreneurs who insist on being paid their full fee can often get the insurance company to agree to do so or, at least, find a mutually agreeable fee somewhere in the middle.

Utilization Reviews

Utilization Reviews (URs) are often, but not always, requested by and performed by third-party payers. At the bottom line, a UR is an audit that determines how well what has been done aligns with what was supposed to have been done. For example, some insurance companies do not pay for diagnostic studies for disorders they believe can be diagnosed solely on clinical examination. A UR study might, for example, look at how many patients with a clinically diagnosable disorder received diagnostic studies even when the insurer's medical necessity criteria say that such studies are unnecessary. Savvy Healthcare Entrepreneurs and healthcare facilities often perform their own URs in the service of quality control and regulatory or contractual compliance.

WHAT IS HEALTH INSURANCE?

In theory, health insurance is simply a risk-sharing agreement between the insured and the insurer. The insured pays the insurer a premium in exchange for which the insurer agrees to absorb some, or all, of the financial burden associated with a healthcare bill. Buyers of health insurance policies are essentially betting that their healthcare bills will be greater than the cost of the policy they buy.

Although this risk-sharing description of health insurance is accurate, an insurance policy is better understood as an investment instrument held by the investors in the insurance company. Using actuaries to guide and shape their policies, these investors, like most businesspeople, seek to generate as much profit as possible at the least expense.

Much of the profit comes from the insurance company's ability to invest the premiums their customers pay until the money is needed to pay a claim. Accordingly, there is a strong financial incentive to discourage people from filing claims and to delay paying claims that are filed. Any unpaid claims result in still more profits. This means that the financial incentives are also lined up to motivate the rejection of claims.

Tactics such as excluding services, excluding diagnoses, adding high deductibles, and using negotiated fee reductions are used to improve the value of the insurance company's investment portfolios.

Patients and some professionals can be confused by the myriad of organizational structures the insurance industry uses to achieve various goals or escape various legislated requirements. In the early days of insurance, the company that sold an insurance policy was usually the same company that processed and paid claims. Nowadays, many insurers outsource the claims management function to any of several types of managed care organizations (MCOs). When this is the case, yet another entity enters the picture, further complicating the relationships between patients and those who provide care.

INSURANCE INDUSTRY ORGANIZATIONAL STRUCTURES

Indemnity Plans

Traditionally, health insurance plans served to indemnify their customers from losses due to healthcare costs. As a group, these plans tend to have the fewest restriction. Due mainly to their expensive premiums, indemnity plans are becoming increasingly rare. They do, however, exist.

With an indemnity plan, the patient's relationship with the insurer is that of a customer. The patient may choose their healthcare providers, so the Healthcare

Entrepreneur may have no relationship with the insurance company when working with a patient who has such a plan. Thus, the Healthcare Entrepreneur–patient relationship (in the traditional sense of the term) can remain just that: a relationship between a healthcare professional and their patient.

Logically, when there is no relationship between the Healthcare Entrepreneur and the insurance company, payments from the insurance company should go directly to the insured patient. The patient can then use that money to reimburse themselves for the money they paid for services at the time the services were rendered. This straightforward model works well when the patient can afford to pay the costs of their care and wait for reimbursement. The model promotes the traditional boundaries of a Healthcare Entrepreneur-patient relationship.

The Healthcare Entrepreneur–patient relationship takes on a new dimension if the Healthcare Entrepreneur accepts the patient's insurance "on assignment." In that case, the Healthcare Entrepreneur becomes their patient's creditor. Moreover, since insurers do not pay every claim that they receive, the Healthcare Entrepreneur who accepts assignment is thereby sharing risk with their patient. The addition of these new dimensions necessarily alters the clinical relationship between the Healthcare Entrepreneur and their patient. Nonetheless, accepting assignment has become a common practice which most patients must expect.

Accepting assignment also creates a de facto relationship of a payer to a payee between the insurance company and the Healthcare Entrepreneur. Once this relationship is established, insurers make demands and insist on concessions in exchange for payment.

For example, indemnity plans typically pay what the insurance industry labels as the "usual and customary" (U&C) fee for a covered service. Almost invariably, that amount is well below the amount typically charged by most professionals rendering the same service. So, even when the insurance company does make a payment, there is almost always a balance of the bill that remains unpaid by the insurer. By accepting assignment, you agree to accept the amount the insurance pays as payment in full. You cannot bill the patient for the difference between what you charged and what the insurance company pays. In effect, by accepting assignment you have agreed to reduce your fee.

If you do not accept assignment, you remain free to bill the patients for the balance left on their account after the insurance company has made its' payment. This is a practice known as "balance billing." Unless you have accepted assignment, there is no prohibition against charging the remainder of the bill to the patient.

Managed Care Organizations

Conceptually, Managed Care Organizations (MCOs) are formed to contain healthcare costs. Their success in doing so over the decades is questionable. Regardless of whether they are owned by an insurance company or are truly free-standing entities, MCOs strive for cost containment. Toward that end, they use tactics such as limiting provider fees, limiting patient access to specialized care, and discouraging service usage that they deem to be not medically necessary.

Joining an insurance network and signing an agreement with an MCO are matters to be taken seriously. The contracts tend to be quite lengthy, somewhat confusing, and slanted against your best interests. Although there is some room to negotiate some of the terms of some of the contracts, doing so can be a time-consuming challenge that can take months to complete.

Several common clauses in these contracts are so surprising that many healthcare professionals incorrectly insist that they cannot be enforced. For example, many contracts allow the insurance company to change significant portions of the contract simply by notifying the professional they are doing so.

Another surprising clause allows the insurance company to sell or lease their networks to other MCOs. When this occurs, Healthcare Entrepreneurs may find that they now must learn the parameters and requirements of an entity that has some control over their practice but with whom they have never had direct dealings.

Health Maintenance Organizations

Perhaps because of its name, the Health Maintenance Organization (HMO) model is often misunderstood by patients and professionals alike. At its core, the model calls for patients to choose a primary care physician who will serve, in addition to other roles, as the gatekeeper of the patient's access to services outside of the primary care doctor's office.

In this model, patients who wish to use their insurance must see their primary care physician (PCP) and obtain a referral before seeing specialists or seeking other services. HMOs reduce overall healthcare costs by limiting the pool of available professionals to those who will follow the often-quite-restrictive protocols promulgated by the HMO, and accept discounted fees.

The Health Maintenance Organization Act of 1973 mandates that employers offering health insurance benefits to employee pools of 25 or more must include an HMO option in their offerings. Some states have laws that further control HMOs, noteworthy among which are those prohibiting nonparticipating professionals from billing patients directly for services that the patient's HMO would cover if the patient sought services within the HMO's network. In other words, some jurisdictions have laws on the books that effectively block Healthcare Entrepreneurs from working with a subset of possible patients, at least if they want to be paid for providing their services.

Healthcare Entrepreneurs in specialties outside of primary care can find themselves unwittingly involved in an HMO model. For example, many hospitals have contracts with HMOs. An inpatient covered by an HMO who is admitted to the hospital may have limits on what services will be covered. Consulting professionals who are not recognized and preapproved by the HMO may find themselves unable to successfully bill for the services they render in the hospital or as part of post-discharge aftercare. A variant of this occurs when a physician-hospital organization (PHO) to which a specialist belongs signs an agreement with an HMO, binding the specialist to HMO terms unless the specialist explicitly opts out.

Regardless of specialty or field, Healthcare Entrepreneurs should make informed, thoughtful decisions before involving themselves in the HMO model. Because the model calls for most issues to be addressed in the primary care office, patients who are referred to other resources may, as a group, to be sicker and in more need of professional time than others.

Opting out of an HMO does not always sufficiently protect professionals from having responsibilities to HMO patients. Office procedures should be in place to ensure that HMO patients are identified before services are rendered. Even then, problems can arise when an existing patient changes insurance to an HMO plan or when a valued referral source refers a patient who is insured in an HMO plan.

Preferred Provider Organizations

Preferred Provider Organizations (PPOs) place more of the gatekeeping function in the hands of the insured patient. Under such plans, patients essentially agree to seek all their nonemergency healthcare services from professionals and facilities that have contracts with the insurer. Those professionals and facilities are referred to as being "in-network." All other professionals, as well as other facilities, are considered "out-of-network."

Some PPO plans take no responsibility for payment for services rendered out of network. Other PPO plans allow the patients they insure to see professionals who are out of network. These plans tend to be costlier and often are structured to discourage using this option by assigning higher deductibles and higher copays when out-of-network services are used. As a rule of thumb, when working with a patient as an out-of-network Healthcare Entrepreneur, have the patient pay for your services at the time they are rendered. The patient can then seek reimbursement from their insurer.

Exclusive Provider Organizations

Exclusive Provider Organizations (EPOs) are a hybrid of the PPO and HMO plans. Patients in EPOs typically are free to seek services from anyone they choose from within an established, limited network of professionals who have agreed to the fee schedules and contract terms laid out by the EPO. In this model, the patient is also free to choose their own primary care physician. In other words, the patient retains the right to be the gatekeeper controlling their access to specialists. The trade-off is that the pool of eligible specialists tends to be limited.

When a patient and the treating professional are both tied to the same network, there should be few surprises, as, at least in theory, both have read, understood, and agreed to comply with the network's contract terms and fee schedules. On the other hand, when a patient seeks services from an out-of-network professional, the professional must take additional steps to ensure that payment will be received. For example, it is especially important to confirm the terms of the patient's policy. Many insurance plans have two different deductibles: one for in-network services and one for out-of-network services. Because insurance plans can be confusing, patients sometimes honestly report that they have met their deductible, forgetting that they have not met their out-of-network deductible.

Likewise, where a copayment or coinsurance is necessary, patients may honestly believe that they are being asked to pay a higher copay than specified in the policy. As proof, they may point to the in-network amount printed on the insurance card. The out-of-network amount is not always printed on the card. It is incumbent on the Healthcare Entrepreneur or a staff member to know the correct amount to charge in each circumstance. Failure to do so can result in ill will, unnecessary billing expenses, and, possibly, nonpayment.

Every Healthcare Entrepreneur must understand and keep track of their relationships with the insurance industry. Like it or not, the insurance industry wields tremendous influence over healthcare policies, healthcare economics, and healthcare competition. Healthcare Entrepreneurs who wish to insulate themselves from these influences must close the door on the insurance industry and build their practices on a strictly fee-for-service basis.

The Cash Flow Cycle

The flow of money through your practice is analogous to the flow of blood through your body. When the flow of money is slowed or stopped, bad things happen. The cash flow cycle includes every step necessary to ensure that money flows smoothly into your practice and ultimately into your pocket. This section focuses on the cash flow cycle and the procedures needed to keep the cash flowing.

BILLING AND COLLECTIONS

Before exploring the cash flow cycle in healthcare, it may be helpful to consider cash flow cycles in other businesses. In many business transactions, a consumer pays for and receives a product or a service from a vendor. There is no need for the vendor to record more than two pieces of information: the charge and the payment.

This transaction can become significantly more complicated if the vendor agrees to bill the consumer for the services rendered or product sold and accept payments over time until the bill is paid in full. In this case, the vendor must obtain and record a great deal of information about the consumer, such as billing addresses and, if the anticipated bill is substantial, information about the consumer's creditworthiness. The vendor then must enter the charges and send a bill. If the bill is not paid promptly, the vendor must send subsequent bills. Each time a payment is made, the payment must be recorded. All of these extra steps take time and are costly to the vendor.

In healthcare, at least when third-party payers are involved, the circumstances are even more complicated. The vendor (e.g., Healthcare Entrepreneur) must obtain and record a great deal about the patient, including the patient's insurance policies and billing address. The vendor must then confirm that the insurance will cover the planned services.

When the patient is seen, charges must be entered along with copayments and any coinsurances collected. Then, the vendor must bill the insurance company in hopes of payment. If the initial claim is rejected, it must be revised and resubmitted. If and when the primary insurance has paid their portion, the remaining bill may need to be sent to a secondary insurance company or to the patient.

After everyone who is going to pay makes their payments, more time must be spent reviewing and writing off any remaining charges.

Clearly, the system is not designed to be smooth or financially efficient; it is designed to discourage creditors (e.g., Healthcare Entrepreneurs) from pursuing full payment of monies due to them. Knowing how to manage the cash flow cycle can save some of the frustration and loss associated with this unnecessarily complicated process.

Billing and Collections Are Not the Same Thing

The terms "billing" and "collections" are often used interchangeably as though they refer to the same process. Not only are the two processes different, losing sight of the distinction can lead to costly mistakes.

In its most basic form, billing is an informational process — the process by which charges are recorded for the benefit of the seller and invoices are sent to the buyer. No money changes hands in the billing process.

On the other hand, collections is a more active process focused on bringing in or collecting monies due. Sometimes this process is routine, such as when a patient pays their copayment at the window or makes a timely payment in response to a billing statement. Occasionally, collections require multiple efforts using various strategies to obtain payment from a reticent debtor.

Although billing typically precedes collections, that is not always the case. Whenever a deposit is collected or a copayment is made before the patient is seen, collections have preceded billing. Billing and collections, though separate functions, are integrally intertwined. Successes or failures in billing will almost always result in matching successes or failures in collections.

Essential References and Guides for Billing

You will need access to several essential references in order to bill successfully.

Even if you do not accept insurance, you will need to know the appropriate diagnostic and procedural codes with which to describe your work. The comprehensive guide to all healthcare procedures is the Current Procedural Terminology (CPT) manual, which is published annually by the American Medical Association (AMA). The title of each volume typically is the acronym CPT, followed by the year that the specific volume addresses. Each edition is available in both a standard edition, which covers just the basics, and a professional edition, which provides a more in-depth view. Each edition is costly to purchase, so it's fortunate that some professional societies publish advisories and articles to keep their members up to date on the CPT codes that are relevant for the specialties they serve. Every practice should have the most up-to-date version of either a specialty guide or the complete compendium.

Evaluation and Management (E/M) codes are among those listed in the CPT. The E/M codes distinguish between types of patients (i.e. new or established), places of service (i.e. inpatient, outpatient), levels of complexity of the service provided, and the amount of time spent providing that service. Physicians, Nurse Practitioners, Clinical Nurse Specialists, Certified Nurse Midwives, And Physician Assistants use E/M codes. As of this writing, no other professionals are paid according to these codes, at least by Medicare or Medicaid. Those who are eligible to bill E/M codes are likely to find that doing so significantly enhances the remunerative value of time spent with patients.

Another essential reference is the most current edition of the International Classification of Diseases and Related Health Problems (ICD), which is published by the World Health Organization (WHO). Printed editions can be purchased from major booksellers. Free online access to the current edition of the ICD is available through the WHO (www.WHO.int) and the Centers for Medicare & Medicaid Services (www.CMS.gov) websites.

The Healthcare Common Procedure Coding System (HCPCS) is another coding system that has gone through several transformations since it was introduced in 1978. These alphabetically coded healthcare procedures range from A (for transportation services, medical supplies, and other items) through V (for vision and hearing services). Some of the codes apply to hard products such as durable medical equipment (E), while other codes apply to medical services (M). Although relatively few Healthcare Entrepreneurs need to use HCPCS codes, some do.

TIP: Remember that the patient may not be the same as the person who actually subscribes to the insurance policy being used. For example, a child may be the patient and the parent is the subscriber. Make sure the right names, birthdates, and genders appear in the right places in your claims.

BILLING PROCEDURES

The cash flow cycle begins with the first contact with a patient. Thinking through the steps from a patient's first call to your receipt of payment will help you develop effective procedures to ensure that all the money due to you is collected and deposited.

Whether the first contact is initiated by the patient or by a referral source, it is essential to get the complete and accurate information needed to generate successful insurance claims and other forms of billing. When data are missing, inaccurate, or incomplete, it is not possible to generate what is called a "clean claim." Clean claims are those that meet all of the criteria the payer insists be met before they will adjudicate the claim. Insurance companies invariably will reject claims they deem not clean. Although you can sometimes clean up and resubmit the claim, doing so is time-consuming, expensive, and further delays payment.

Collecting this important information may seem like a straightforward process, and most of the time, it is. There are several common pitfalls to be aware of, however. For example, consider the patient who registers as Barb Anderson but is registered with her insurance company as Barbara Anderson. Claims submitted using the name Barb are likely to be rejected. Likewise, consider the effects of a simple typographical error if the data entry clerk types in Ms. Anderson's name as Barbara Aderson.

Addresses that are reported inaccurately or recorded inaccurately create problems as well. For example, some patients carefully and accurately report the legal name of the city in which they live when applying for insurance but use the name of their neighborhood when completing less-formal documents. The mismatch can stop an insurance claim in its tracks even though all of the other information points to the correct patient.

> **TIP:** When patients are seen in hospitals and other institutional settings, the face sheet containing all the information needed for a clean claim should be obtained from the patient's hospital chart. This often can be accomplished by logging into the hospital's electronic records and downloading the needed information. When that is not possible, staff members at the hospital unit are often quite willing to send the information via fax.

Omissions and errors can interfere with successful billing. A claim submitted to an insurer with missing fields of information is sure to be rejected. A claim sent to the wrong address, be it an electronic or physical address, may simply be ignored by the company that receives it. Since some insurers have different subsets of claims processed by different departments or other companies, it is easier than you might think to send a claim to the wrong address.

Use an intake form to collect all of the information needed to bill and collect from both the patient and the insurer. The form can be on paper or it can be the template that your billing program uses when a new patient is registered. Forms also can be emailed to a prospective patient, or posted on your website and in the patient portal so that patients can complete them in advance. Using these forms ensures that nothing has been forgotten.

Remember, however, that forms do not prevent transcription errors. So, best practices are to either electronically scan or take a photocopy of both sides of the patient's driver's license and insurance card and compare the information to the information that was entered into your billing program to ensure they match.

The Minimum Data Set for Successful Billing

The paper version of the universal billing form for most outpatient healthcare services is known as the HCFA 1500 form (see Form 1). HCFA stands for the Health Care Financing Administration, which is now known as the Centers for Medicare & Medicaid Services (CMS). Most commercial insurers insist that they be billed using this form. Electronic billing programs are written to include the elements of the HCFA 1500. Items 1–13 of the form include information the patient should provide if they want you to bill their insurance.

Before Your Patient Arrives

Before a patient arrives in your office, verify their insurance coverage. This can be accomplished most efficiently by going to the appropriate insurance verification website, as was discussed in Chapter 2. Many medical billing programs offer a feature that conducts the insurance verification for a fee.

Because the information posted online by insurance companies and their agents can be notoriously error-prone, some Healthcare Entrepreneurs prefer to confirm benefits by telephone. This is a costly process, often marked by long periods of time during which the caller is left on hold. The decision to use telephone calls rather than online searches to confirm benefits should be based on a cost-benefit analysis. That is, if the financial loss associated with incorrect information provided online exceeds the cost of having someone call to check benefits, then the telephone system makes sense. Otherwise, internet-based benefit checks are in order.

There are several things to check when confirming insurance coverage. First, since insurance coverage sometimes lapses, confirm that the prospective patient is still

Form 1. Health Insurance Claim Form HCFA 1500

insured. Knowing when the current policy is scheduled to lapse lets you know when to check to confirm that the patient has, in fact, renewed the same policy.

Likewise, it is important to find out whether there is a deductible associated with the policy. If there is a deductible, knowing the dollar amount of the deductible and how much of that amount has already been met is essential. When a deductible has not yet been fully met, the insurance company will not make a payment. In such cases, the patient should be required to pay prior to or at the time of service, even if they insist that the insurance company's information is not accurate. If, in fact, the patient is correct, the patient can recoup the resulting overpayment from the insurer. If, on the other hand, the deductible has not been met, collecting payments from that patient can be particularly challenging unless done in advance.

Next, find out about any policy restrictions. You don't need to read each patient's insurance policy in its entirety. These restrictions are typically available on the insurer's website. Some of the restrictions fly in the face of common sense, so be sure that the policy terms you have read truly address the services you plan to render. For example, some policies cover services rendered in a hospital but do not cover those same services when they are rendered in an outpatient office or another setting.

A key component of the benefits check is to learn which expenses the patient will be responsible for, such as deductibles, copayments, coinsurance, and other out-of-pocket expenses. Knowing this allows you to collect the right amounts at the time of service and prevents unnecessary billing costs.

Once benefits have been confirmed, obtain approval for the specific procedures planned for the patient. This involves precertification, preauthorization, or both. There are several routes through which precertification and preauthorization can be accomplished, including telephone inquiries, faxed requests, and internet requests.

It is important to be specific about your request. Any error or omission in what you tell the insurance company you want to be approved can invalidate the approval after you have rendered the service. Obtain and record an authorization number, along with the date and the name of the person who provided the number. That number will be needed to complete a clean claim and should be entered in HCFA 1500 line 23 or its electronic equivalent.

> **TIP:** Some, but not all, superbills show the fee for each procedure. This makes it easier for the clinician or a clerk to calculate the cost of the visit and collect fees from the patients at check out.

It is a good idea to insist that the certification or authorization be approved in writing. Some insurance companies refuse to do so on the grounds that written approval is unnecessary. They may be correct, since most written approval letters include some language reserving the insurance company's right to refuse payment despite the prior authorization. Nonetheless, whenever possible, get it in writing.

Billing – The Back-Office View

Each of the steps in the billing process that have been discussed thus far can and, in most circumstances, should be handled by front-office personnel. The next steps in the billing process are typically performed by clinicians who provide information to billing specialists working in what is known as the "back office."

Forms used to record the information needed to complete the second half of the HCFA 1500 form are referred to as "superbills" or "encounter forms." A well-designed superbill, be it in electronic or paper form, provides clinicians with checklists with which they can document the procedures they provided and the diagnoses that justified each procedure. This information is used to fill in item 24 of the HCFA 1500 form.

Most of the remaining information needed for the HCFA 1500 form can be pre-printed on the superbill. This includes information such as the clinician's name, credentials, NPI number and address; the patient's name and date of birth; the date services are rendered; and the federal Tax Identification Number (TIN) of the billing entity since the billing entity is not always the same as the clinician. Although some Healthcare Entrepreneurs have their signatures preprinted on their superbills, best practices dictate that each superbill be signed only after it is completed.

Superbills can be structured to accomplish more than the basic task of recording and reporting new fees to be charged. For example, collections of monies due at the check-in or check-out window can be facilitated by printing the patient's current account balance and copayment amounts on the superbill.

Another modification helps Healthcare Entrepreneurs efficiently document the next steps in each patient's care by leaving room to record when the patient's next appointment should be, what diagnostic work should be arranged, and what referrals should be made. The person who checks out the patient can use this information to make the appropriate arrangements.

When a superbill is printed on paper, the information it contains must be transcribed into electronic form if the billing is to be sent out electronically. This task is typically performed by a billing specialist but can be done by others. The cost of transcription errors is high because the costs of locating the error and re-billing are high. So, it is often more cost-efficient for billing specialists and transcriptionists to double-check their entries before finalizing them. By keeping track of the frequency and costs of re-billings in your practice, you can determine the cost-benefit ratio of spending time double-checking data entries.

> **TIP:** The terms "invoice" and "statement" often are misused interchangeably. An invoice puts the responsible party on notice that they have an obligation to pay. A statement summarizes the transactions recorded in an account.

Taken together, the information from the superbill plus the information collected from each patient prior to each encounter provides the data needed to generate a bill. In cases where insurance is not involved, an invoice should be generated and sent to the person who is responsible for making payments. The "responsible party" is not always the patient. For example, parents are most often the responsible party on accounts in which the patient is a minor.

When insurance is involved, claims should be prepared and sent electronically or on the HCFA 1500 form discussed above. Most of the claims that are sent electronically are routed through a clearinghouse to which your billing software is connected. In a process known as "scrubbing," the clearinghouse electronically scans each claim for identifiable flaws. When a flaw is detected, the clearinghouse will return the claim to you for correction. The clearinghouse forwards claims that make it through the scrubbing process to the identified payer.

Some insurance companies have websites at which claims can be entered directly. In this case, the insurer processes the claim. Flaws in the claim trigger a rejection. Claims that are rejected or denied will have to be corrected and resubmitted.

COLLECTIONS

The term "collections" has developed a negative undertone, connotating a somewhat adversarial process in which a creditor attempts to pry payments loose from the hands of a resistant debtor. In fact, the term has a much broader meaning, referring to any of several activities in which money is transferred from a payer to a payee. Adversarial processes are rarely needed when the billing process is done well.

How Money Flows In

Patients make payments in any of several ways; each has its advantages and disadvantages. Some patients may choose to pay via your patient portal if the portal is set up to tell them their balance and accept payment. This is an efficient means of receiving payments and involves little or no staff time. In contrast, when patients come to your office to make payments or call to pay by credit card, they add traffic that can slow the processing of other patients.

Payments made by mail can be processed efficiently, although sometimes the payer neglects to identify which account to which the payment should be applied. Therefore, it is helpful to include a payment stub on your billing invoices.

When Your Patient Arrives

With benefits confirmed and precertification/preauthorization accomplished, you can see your patient and expect to get paid for doing so. Armed with the knowledge obtained during the benefits check, you or your staff can request and receive payment from the patient. Unless you require an advanced deposit from your patients, this is the first step in the collections process.

The question of when to have patients pay is a matter of preference and is often based on factors such as the flow of patient traffic through the check-in and check-out processes combined with considerations such as whether the patient's financial responsibility is fixed or variable. As a rule, the sooner the money is collected, the better.

The relationship between a patient and their Healthcare Entrepreneur should not be clouded by issues of indebtedness. Patients who say "I forgot my checkbook" should be asked to pay by credit card. Nearly every American has at least one credit card; those who do not have one may not be creditworthy. When someone insists that they have no way to make payment at or before the time of services, you should have established procedures designed to limit the likelihood that you will become your patient's creditor. Beware the temptation to refuse further services until the payment is received. Issues of patient abandonment must be considered and managed appropriately.

Many insurance policies designate a specific flat copayment amount to be charged at each patient encounter. In these cases, payment should be obtained before the patient is seen. Like it or not, there are "drive-offs" in healthcare practices — patients who, having received services, leave the office without paying. This creates unnecessary collections expenses and bad debts.

Collecting payments at check-in is a bit more challenging when the insurance policy includes variable costs. An example is a policy that requires the patient to pay 20% of the amount charged rather than a fixed copayment amount per visit. Sometimes there is no way to know in advance what the charges will be for a given visit. Typically, the cost of the basic visit can be anticipated in advance, but the need for other services such as injections may not be known until well after the patient has checked in.

One way to address this situation is to ask for payment as the patient checks out. Another way is to obtain the predictable amount at check-in and then, at check-out, remind the patient that additional services were received, necessitating an additional payment. The cost of collecting money after a patient has left your office versus collecting twice in one visit should be considered when determining your window collections procedures.

Cash Payments. More often than not, the patient is the one who makes the first payment for a rendered service. Sometimes, patients want to pay in cash, which is a mixed blessing. Certainly, it is desirable to accept as many forms of payment as possible to make it easy for patients to pay at the time service is rendered. However, there is an increased risk of theft when cash is involved. Daily anti-theft audits can be helpful, but by the time theft is discovered, it may be too late to do much about it; the money is gone.

The simplest form of cash theft involves an employee who removes some cash from the day's receipts with no effort to cover the action. Having a person who does not routinely handle receipts tally up the amount of revenue brought in each day and match the total to the amount of the bank deposit and the amount expected can help reduce this sort of theft.

Unfortunately, some thieves are more sophisticated and cover their tracks with tactics such as voiding a charge or designating an account as closed. To limit the options and temptations for these thieves, insist that everyone who pays in cash is provided with a receipt from the person accepting the cash. Signs directing patients to always insist on a receipt will help reduce the potential for theft.

Payment by Check. Of the various forms of payment, checks are among the most desirable because it is more difficult for thieves to steal checks made out to the practice than it is to steal cash. This does not mean that checks cannot or will not be stolen by an unscrupulous employee. For example, the employee receiving the check may offer to save the patient time by using a rubber stamp to fill in the name of the practice to which the check is being tendered. After the patient has gone, the thief fills in their own name instead.

Employees who receive payments in any form should be required to log each payment immediately. If the payment is in the form of a check, the recipient should immediately stamp the back of the check with the words For Deposit Only: Account Number (insert your business checking account number).

Payment by Credit Card. There are pros and cons to accepting credit cards as a form of payment in your practice. As discussed in Chapter 1, accepting payment by credit card creates an elective expense to your practice. The so-called "discount rates" — the amount the credit card vendor charges you — can be steep.

On the other hand, credit cards are ubiquitous. Many patients prefer to pay by credit card so they can collect as many credit card rewards points as possible or so they can have a record of every expenditure they make. Therefore, choosing not to accept credit cards risks losing these patients. Conversely, practices that do accept credit cards offer an attractive "customer service" to their patients.

Not all credit card transactions are the same. There are important differences between transactions in which the card itself was used to pay a bill and those in which the card number is manually entered using the information on file. For example, the fee you pay for a transaction in which the card was not present often is higher than the fee for the same transaction completed with the actual card.

> **TIP:** Protecting patients from identity theft due to data leakage involves more than protecting computers from hackers. Staff members' access to sensitive information should be limited to "need to know."

It is more difficult for a patient to successfully dispute a charge when their card was presented to make a payment. When a card number is entered manually, the burden will fall on the Healthcare Entrepreneur to prove that a card holder's disputed charge was valid and authorized. To keep this problem to a minimum, always have patients sign a credit card authorization form before accepting payment by telephone or charging a credit card that the patient left with you on file.

Credit card information should be handled in a secure manner that ensures the information will remain confidential and your patients are protected from identity theft. In essence, it is best to treat such information with the same care as you would treat Protected Health Information (PHI) under HIPAA. The Payment Card Industry Security Standards Council has standards by which this can be achieved, and liability can be managed. Most, but not all, medical billing software is written to protect credit card information.

Credit as a Form of Payment. Healthcare Entrepreneurs sometimes choose to serve patients who cannot afford to pay; the decision to do so might involve a complete write-off of the fees. In such cases, the services are said to have been rendered "pro bono." Pro bono services should be recorded in the patient's clinical record and billing record and then the charges should be written off. Since no money has changed hands, you cannot write off such charitable acts as income tax deductions.

On occasion, a patient can afford the care they need only if they can pay the fee later or over time. Any Healthcare Entrepreneur who agrees to such an arrangement becomes a creditor, much like a bank. As a creditor, you should obtain a written agreement to pay. Such an agreement should address state, local, and federal legal requirements. It should specify the dollar amount of the credit you are extending, the schedule by which payment is promised, the interest rate to be charged, late payment fees, if any, and the jurisdiction in which disputes involving the agreement will be heard.

Letters of Protection

Sometimes Healthcare Entrepreneurs are asked to diagnose or treat patients who are involved in litigation, such as a patient who was injured in an automobile accident. When the patient is unable or unwilling to pay for your services, the patient's Attorney may offer a Letter of Protection (LOP) instead of immediate payment. LOPs are promises to pay for services previously rendered from the proceeds of a pending lawsuit.

LOPs can be fraught with problems because they are promises to pay, not guarantees of payment. Most often, payment is contingent on the patient winning their lawsuit, so accepting a LOP makes you an unwitting stakeholder in the lawsuit. As a stakeholder, your credibility as a witness will likely be questioned if you are subpoenaed to testify in the matter.

Even if the suit is won, Attorneys do not always remember to pay. Lawsuits can drag on for years, so the holder of a LOP must frequently check on the status of the lawsuit by sending letters to the Attorney or by checking online. Virtually all judicial circuits have websites on which the status of cases being heard can be tracked. Locate these websites with a simple internet search using terms such as "Clerk of the Court (insert the name of your county) Court Case Search."

PAYMENTS FROM INSURANCE COMPANIES

Payments from insurance companies and other third-party payers can arrive via different routes. Some payers still send paper checks in the mail; a few payers send credit cards, which the recipient must then withdraw the money from. Most third-party payments are made electronically by transferring money from one bank account to another. These are known as Electronic Funds Transfers (EFTs).

TIP: Some insurance companies attempt to pay claims by issuing a credit card that they simply print onto their Explanation of Benefits. These can easily be overlooked by a busy billing clerk. Some of these cards have a fee associated with cashing them. Healthcare Entrepreneurs should refuse to accept this form of payment.

Explanations of Benefits and Electronic Remittance Advice

When an insurance company processes a claim, the insurer's conclusions about that claim are most commonly documented using an Explanation of Benefits (EOB), or an Electronic Remittance Advice (ERA). EOBs typically arrive in the mail; ERAs can be viewed through your billing software or on the payer's website. Regardless of the name of the form or the mode of delivery, these documents inform you of how the claim was processed, albeit in cryptic form. They also let you know what portions of the claim will be paid, what portions should be collected from the patient or secondary insurer, what portions of the claim are being denied, and, in coded form, the reasons for any denials. Sometimes the payment accompanies these documents; at other times, the money arrives separately and must be matched to the EOB or ERA.

When EOBs or ERAs arrive separately from the payments they describe, it is usually best to wait until you have both the money and the EOB or ERA in hand before recording the payment. Money can slip through the cracks if the reported payment is recorded before the actual money is in the bank.

Too often, those who receive and process this information are undertrained or overworked. So, they may unquestioningly accept what is written on the form they receive. Doing so can be expensive because EOBs and ERAs can contain significant errors, and many, while accurate, require additional actions to collect all monies due.

> **TIP:** Four entities may be responsible for paying some portion of each bill: (1) the patient may pay some or all of the charge, (2) the insurance company or other third-party payer may pay all or some of the charge, (3) a secondary payer may pay some or all of what the primary insurer did not pay, and (4) in some cases, a portion of the charge may have to be written off as a bad debt or as part of a negotiated fee agreement.

Although interpreting ERAs and EOBs can seem daunting to the uninitiated, much like any foreign language, they become easier to understand the more you work with them. Understanding and responding appropriately to an ERA or EOB is easier if you remember a simple accounting rule: 100% of the amount you originally billed must be accounted for in the EOB or ERA.

All EOBs and ERAs are organized in a tabular format. Each row is dedicated to a specific service billed on a specific date. The first few columns tend to simply repeat the information the biller sent to the insurance company, including the date(s) of service, place of service (because payments may differ based on where services were provided), CPT or other procedure codes for the service that was billed, and the amount charged for the procedure being billed.

The next set of columns typically addresses the payer's conclusions regarding how much they should pay for the billed procedure, how much you should write-off, and how much should be paid by the patient or a secondary payer.

When some or all of the claim is being denied, the denied amount is shown, along with the reasons for the denial. These reasons are expressed in Denial Codes or Reason Codes. Some insurers provide the key to the codes used on each EOB or ERA. Most billing software offers a directory explaining each code. When neither the insurer nor the software explains a given code, the meaning can be found through an internet search.

Perhaps not surprisingly, there are more than 300 Denial Codes. They are clustered in code groups (see Table 7).

TABLE 7. Denial Code Group

Code Group	Code Group Description
CO	Contractual Obligation
CR	Corrections and Reversals
OA	Other Adjustment
PI	Payer Initiated Reductions
PR	Patient Responsibility

The most common denial codes are labeled with the code group name, followed by the numeric identifier for the specific code. For example, PR1 is the code used when the insurer believes the patient has not yet met their policy's deductible, so the patient is responsible for the denied amount.

> **TIP:** Contractual Obligation denial codes can be avoided by researching the limits and exclusions of each patient's insurance policy, knowing and adhering to the payer's "medical necessity" criteria, and seeking precertification before performing a procedure.

The Contractual Obligation (CO) group codes encompass denials for services that are not covered under the patient's insurance plan and the amount you had agreed to write off if and when you agreed to the payer's fee schedule. As a rule, the patient cannot be billed for these amounts. There are circumstances in which a CO denial can be appealed, such as when the insurer deems the charge to be "not medically necessary."

In most jurisdictions, insurers have the right to "look back" over claims they have previously processed and change their minds. When the payer believes they overpaid, they recapture the money using Corrections and Reversals (CR) codes. Even when the correction or reversal is applied to one patient's claims, the money often will be withheld from another patient's claim. For example, if the insurer believes they overpaid you $100 when they paid Mr. Smith's previous claim, and they believe they should pay you $250 for Ms. Jones' current claim, they may send you only $150 for services to Ms. Jones.

Typically, insurance companies will notify you to request that you issue a refund before they recoup monies through a reversal. When this occurs, it is often prudent to issue a refund even if you do not believe it is due because the bookkeeping will become a bit of a nightmare if the insurer withholds the money from a payment for a different patient's claim. When the amount of the refund justifies taking the time to do so, you can try to recapture the refund by appealing the insurer's decision.

> **TIP:** When a refund is due to a patient, offer them the opportunity to keep the refund amount as a credit against future charges. Maintaining and then applying a credit is more efficient than writing a refund check.

Claims rejected using Payer Initiated Reductions (PI) codes deserve special attention. These codes are used when the payer, without a contractual basis that would otherwise justify a rejection, decides that a claim should be rejected. This can be a unilateral decision without a contractual underpinning. So, unless the amount at risk is too small to justify the time, PI rejections should be evaluated as cases to be appealed.

> **TIP:** OA rejections should routinely be appealed using a form letter that includes a demand for payment or a proper explanation.

With more than 300 Denial Codes to choose from, you might think there would be no need for an Other Adjustment (OA) category. Nonetheless, there is such a category, and it is used, all too frequently, when none of the other 300 Denial Codes apply. OA rejections are particularly problematic for billing personnel since they tend to be ambiguous. Billing specialists must study the claim in search of an error or problem.

Coordination of Benefits

When the patient has more than one insurance policy, there may be a Coordination of Benefits (COB) between the primary and the secondary payers. As the term implies, this involves the primary insurer communicating directly with the secondary insurer to ensure complete payment of allowed amounts. In many jurisdictions, Medicare automatically coordinates benefits with many secondary payers so that a claim is forwarded to the secondary payer with no further action needed by you.

When COB does not occur, you must file a second claim with the secondary payer for the unpaid portions of the bill. If there is no secondary payer, you should collect the remaining portion of the "allowed amount" from the patient. The allowed amount is shown on the EOB, or ERA. Obviously, payment is significantly slowed by a process in which you must wait for one payer to process your claim before you can seek payment for the remainder from another payer. Payment can be further slowed when, as is often the case, the secondary payer refuses to process the claim until they are provided with the EOB from the primary payer. It is sometimes necessary to revert to paper claims so the primary payer's EOB can be enclosed. Sometimes, the amount at stake is less than the cost of billing the secondary, in which case the option of writing off the remaining charge deserves consideration.

Successful Collections from Insurance Companies

In theory, a clean claim should result in a timely payment from the third-party payer. When such a payment has been made, the payment should be entered into the patient's account and credited to the specific charge that is being paid. This system not only makes it easier to respond to questions about an account, but it also provides you with information you will need to pursue claims that have been underpaid and claims that are past due.

In some circumstances, such as a boutique massage therapy practice, Healthcare Entrepreneurs choose to simply apply payments to a running balance. This system requires less data entry time than a system in which payments are matched to charges. Nonetheless, this "running ledger" approach is not recommended for most Healthcare Entrepreneurs because it is not conducive to successful collections in practices that pursue payments from insurance companies.

Once payments have been recorded, the amount due is reduced in the patient's ledger. Sometimes, a portion of the original bill remains unpaid in the ledger. This can be due to any of a number of factors, but typically, the amount remaining is the difference between the amount billed and the agreed-upon fee as negotiated with the insurance company. In such cases, the unpaid amount should be adjusted off the patient's account with the notation that the adjustment is due to a negotiated fee.

COLLECTING PAST-DUE ACCOUNTS

No matter how assiduously you follow the billing and collections steps discussed above, there will be times when monies due you are not paid in a timely manner.

Past-Due Insurance Claims

When a claim remains unpaid by an insurance company, it is often worthwhile to call that company's claims department. Although the primary purpose of the call is to get the claim paid in full, there are other objectives as well, including learning what aspect of your practice's billing procedures resulted in a problem with payment. You can use this knowledge to correct claims and amend procedures to prevent the problem from recurring.

Some jurisdictions have laws governing the prompt payment of claims. It behooves every Healthcare Entrepreneur to be familiar with such laws if they exist in their jurisdiction. It is also important to know how much time your contracts with each insurer allow for the claim to be "processed." Such knowledge helps guide policies such as when to start investigating and pursuing an insurance claim and when to allow the insurance company more time to process the claim.

Even in this age of electronic billing, some claims get "lost." It is helpful to be able to track a claim before investing the time needed to call the insurer. You can track claims in a number of ways. Some billing software programs offer a claim-tracking feature. Some insurers post the status of a claim on their websites or on websites such as those discussed in Chapter 2. Still others use artificial intelligence automation to respond to claim status inquiries made over the telephone.

Past-Due Patient Balances

Ideally, you will structure your practice's procedures to ensure that all monies due from a patient are paid at the time of service, and all insurance policies have been confirmed. These procedures are essential to minimizing the costs, in both dollars and difficult patient relations, associated with billing for accounts that are past due. No loss prevention strategy is foolproof, however. So, it is necessary to have and adhere to policies and procedures by which past-due accounts are pursued.

> **TIP:** Staff charged with calling insurance companies regarding claims or precertification should have access to two or more telephone lines. Since on-hold times tend to be long when calling about claims or precertification, the staff member can use the two lines to call two companies at once. They can simply hang-up the line on which they are on hold if someone answers the other number called.

When it comes to unpaid bills, the older the bill, the less likely it is to be paid. It is essential to bill promptly and to actively pursue payment from the moment a patients' balance is created. Unpaid medical bills are among the most frequent causes of credit score damage. This means that even well-intentioned people who are usually inclined to pay their bills are defaulting on medical bills.

> **TIP:** Some practices send routine advisory billing statements to the patient while the insurance claim is being processed. Although doing so is expensive, it makes the patient aware that money is still owed for services rendered.

Collections policies should include specific cutoffs below which an unpaid bill is automatically written off as bad debt. It makes little sense to spend costly staff time pursuing a $10 underpayment. A second cutoff should be established based on the costs associated with sending the account to a professional collection agent. If the amount to be collected is less than or close to the fee the collections agent will receive, it may be best to treat the account as a bad debt.

The same principle applies when deciding which accounts will be pursued to the point of litigation. Lawsuits in civil or small claims court are costly in terms of time lost, court fees, and the risk of negative public relations. These costs may not be justified unless the bill is significantly higher than the costs of litigation and the likelihood of collecting is reasonable. Remember, you cannot get blood from a stone. A patient with no money will not pay even when ordered to do so in small claims court.

When a patient has an account balance that is past due, the patient should be re-billed promptly. The longer a patient is allowed to delay paying their bill, the less likely they will pay. Exacerbating this problem is the fact that the amount owed by a patient is not always known until weeks or months after services were delivered. This occurs, for example, when an insurance company declines to pay a claim for services that had been previously approved.

Dunning messages can be printed on invoices sent to the patient to help encourage prompt payment (see Checklist 8). Effective dunning messages inform the patient about the status of their account and prompt them to take action. They should be written in clear, formal terms that are easily understood.

When a patient fails to respond to an invoice, consider calling them. Sometimes, the amount past due is too small to justify the costs in staff time associated with making the call. In such a case, it is financially prudent to write off the past due amount as a bad debt. When a patient is called, the caller should be well trained in and adhere to the laws governing the collections of debts. See Checklist 9 for tips for successful collections calls.

CHECKLIST 8

Sample Dunning Messages and Patient Billing Schedules

Send an initial invoice immediately upon recording a patient's financial obligation.

This bill is your responsibility.
Your insurer has paid all that it believes they are responsible for. If you have questions, please call your insurer.
Please pay the amount shown in full within 10 days.

Send a 1st Past Due Notice 10–14 days after the initial invoice.

As you previously agreed, the amount shown is your responsibility.
Please pay the amount shown in full within 10 days.

Send a 2nd Past Due Notice 10–14 days after the 1st Past Due Notice.

Your personal account balance is now PAST DUE!
Please pay the amount shown in full within 10 days or
Call us at (123) 456-7890 to discuss payment arrangements.

Send a 3rd Past Due Notice 10–14 days after the 2nd Past Due Notice.

Your personal balance is now SERIOUSLY PAST DUE.
IMMEDIATE PAYMENT IS REQUIRED

Send a Final Notice 10–14 days after the 3rd Past Due Notice.

Your account is scheduled to be sent to a collections
agency 10 days from today.
To prevent this from happening call us at (123) 456-7890 or
make immediate payment.

When telephoning a patient, the goal is to have the patient pay the amount due by credit card during the call. When this cannot be achieved, the Patient can be offered a payment plan that includes specific payment amounts and time frames within which payments will be made. There is room to debate whether it is necessary to have the patient countersign the payment plan since they have already demonstrated a willingness to ignore other agreements they have signed. Nonetheless, the verbal agreement should be memorialized in a written payment plan that is sent to the patient to be signed.

CHECKLIST 9

Tips for Successful Collections Calls

✓ Remember, the person you are calling is a patient and most likely a decent human being.

✓ Come on the call as an ally, intent on helping someone solve a problem.

✓ Smiles can be "felt" over the phone. So smile throughout the call.

✓ Address the person by name.

✓ Tell the other person why you are calling. (i.e., "As a courtesy, we always call patients whose accounts are past due. Sometimes, the patient did not receive their billing statement. Did you receive yours?"

✓ In a matter-of-fact and confident tone, ask which credit card they would like to use to make their payment.

✓ Even if the patient balks or gets upset, stay calm and factual.

✓ Ask open-ended questions to learn what is impeding the patient from paying and how they are justifying reneging.

✓ Acknowledge what they say by repeating or summarizing their words back to them.

✓ Enlist them as an ally committed to solving the problem by asking questions such as "How do you think we should proceed?"

✓ If you believe they truly cannot pay over the phone during the call, get a commitment to pay by a certain date and/or to agree to a payment plan.

✓ Reward their commitment and reaffirm the alliance by telling them how glad you are that you can take their account off of the collections list.

When such a promise is made but not kept, the patient's account should be reviewed as a candidate to be turned over to a collections agency. Likewise, when a patient who has been called does not return messages and continues to ignore written correspondence, the behavior indicates that a more aggressive approach to collections will be needed.

Every business should have preset policies and procedures pertaining to collecting debt that is past due. The terms of the collections policy should be communicated to the patient in both the HIPAA Privacy Practices Notice and the patient's signed agreement to abide by the practice's policies. You should have a preexisting relationship with a reputable collections agent who is familiar with the unique demands of and law pertaining to healthcare collections. You should have a signed HIPAA-compliant Business Associate's Agreement in place with any collections agent or agency with whom you plan to work.

When vetting an account for collections, consider several factors beyond the magnitude of the bill and the anticipated cost of pursuing collections, such as the impact on your relationship with the referral source. Sometimes referral sources are blind to or apathetic about how you manage the patients they refer. Other referral sources may be quite protective of their patients. Consider whether the referral source should be contacted before sending a patient's account to collections. Also, consider the public relations implications if the patient reacts by speaking negatively about you in conversations or online.

Once an account is in collections, the relationship with the patient takes on an adversarial tone. For this reason, with rare exceptions, patients whose account has been sent to collections should be administratively discharged and referred to other professionals. Patients deserve to have a positive relationship with the professionals who treat them.

See Checklist 10 for 12 steps for successful collections and Checklist 11 for do's and don'ts when collecting debts.

Tracking Accounts Receivable

The terms "fee for service" and "out of pocket" refer to those circumstances in which the patient makes payments in full prior to or at the time services are rendered. In such circumstances, the entries in the patient's ledger suffice as the record of the transactions. However, when dealing with insured patients and those to whom credit has been extended, money will still be owed you after you have rendered services. The monies still due to you after you have rendered services are called the Accounts Receivable (A/R). Your practice should have someone skilled at and dedicated to maintaining an accurate record of A/R and actively working to bring the monies due to you into your practice's possession. These functions also can be outsourced to billing services.

Most Healthcare Entrepreneurs rely on automated computer programs to manage all aspects of their practice's financial health, including tracking A/R. The A/R report generated by the billing software is the primary guiding force for collections activity. Even if you never intend to perform your own billing functions, you should understand the A/R report and how it is used.

A/R reports sort the balances due from each payer source, be that a patient or a third party, into "buckets." The buckets are based on how long the amount due has been outstanding, most commonly in 30-day increments. The A/R report allows you to readily see which accounts need attention and which are most likely still being processed.

CHECKLIST 10

12 Steps for Successful Collections

✓ Obtain a signed agreement acknowledging financial responsibilities at the time of admission and annually after that.

✓ Confirm the terms and limitations of insurance policy(s) in advance of an appointment.

✓ Obtain any and all required precertifications for services before performing any procedure.

✓ Collect all past due amounts due from patients when they check-in for an appointment.

✓ Collect all amounts due from the patient for services rendered at the time the service(s) are rendered.

✓ All billings should go out the day services are rendered.

✓ Send a gentle reminder letter and re-bill all patient accounts that remain unpaid 10–14 days after services were rendered.

✓ Send a firmer reminder letter and re-bill all patient accounts that remain unpaid 20–28 days after services were rendered.

✓ Follow-up on all insurance claims that remain unpaid 30 days after the services were rendered.

✓ Send a collections warning message, a copy of the signed agreement to pay, and an offer to set up a payment plan to all patients whose accounts remain unpaid 30–42 days after services were rendered.

✓ Send to collections if unpaid 45 days after services were rendered.

✓ Audit the performance of collections personnel at least monthly using pre-determined numeric benchmarks.

Some A/R reports are written on the premise that insurers need time to process each claim, and patients need time to receive and issue bills after they are sent. As is the case in Table 8, these reports start with a "current" bucket. Claims and bills listed in the current bucket require little or no action by the billing specialist. Sophisticated billing software programs allow you to choose how long you want to trust that a claim or bill is in the process of being paid. If, for example, you believe all claims should be paid within 21 days, you can set the software to move claims and bills to the next bucket once the debt has been outstanding for 21 days.

The longer an account remains unpaid, the less likely it will ever be paid, so it is important for billing specialists to work on accounts that have slipped into the second bucket of the A/R report, be that the 0–30 days or 31–60 days bucket.

CHECKLIST 11

A Partial List of Dos And Don'ts When Collecting Debts

CAUTION: There are federal, state and sometimes local laws, as well as ethical prohibitions in some professions, that govern what can and cannot be said or done in the service of collecting a past due bill. The following is a common-sense list of things to remember. This is not a comprehensive list of your legal responsibilities.

DO

    ✓ Advise the debtor that your communication is in the service of collecting a debt.

    ✓ Remind the debtor that any information shared will be used in the service of collecting that debt.

    ✓ State factually the amount owed.

    ✓ Accurately cite the legal commitment the debtor made, if any exists (i.e., Terms of Service Agreement).

    ✓ Offer viable solutions, such as payment plans, by which the debt can be paid.

DO NOT

    ✓ Threaten the debtor.

    ✓ Pretend to represent a government agency.

    ✓ Disrupt the debtor's employment.

    ✓ Harass the debtor.

    ✓ Call the debtor late at night or early in the morning.

    ✓ Get into any struggles with the debtor.

    ✓ Make any misrepresentation.

Likewise, billing specialists should give priority to accounts that have fallen into the 91–120 days and over 120 days columns. These are the accounts that are well on their way to becoming bad debts.

Small, low-volume practices can keep track of their A/R without the aid of computers. In this old-school system, the ledgers of each patient who has an outstanding balance due on their account are filed in chronological order, starting with the date the earliest service was rendered. The person charged with collecting the monies due can then perform the necessary steps to collect the payment on a pre-determined schedule. For example, ledgers that show monies due from a patient for services rendered 10 days ago might trigger a letter or telephone call to the patient. The ledger is then re-filed for follow-up 10 days later.

TABLE 8. Accounts Receivable—Annotated

Patient Name	Current	30 Days	60 Days	90 Days	120 Days	Total	Unapplied	Net Total
Fauci, Anthony	Perhaps this patient got through did not pay their co-payment. Is there a hole in the copay collection system?							
Patient	$50.00	$0.00	$0.00	$0.00	$0.00	$50.00		$50.00
Insurance	$0.00	$0.00	$0.00	$0.00	$0.00	$0.00		$0.00
Total	$50.00	$0.00	$0.00	$0.00	$0.00	$50.00	$0.00	$50.00
Fauchard, Pierre	It looks like this patient's insurance is not paying claims yet the patient is continuing to receive sercices.							
Patient	$0.00	$0.00	$0.00	$0.00	$0.00	$0.00		$0.00
Insurance	$100.00	$100.00	$0.00	$100.00	$300.00	$600.00		$600.00
Total	$100.00	$0.00	$0.00	$0.00	$0.00	$600.00	$0.00	$600.00
Freud, Sigmund	This claim was recently submitted and has not yet been paid. No action needed right now.							
Patient	$0.00	$0.00	$0.00	$0.00	$0.00	$0.00		$0.00
Insurance	$1,405.00	$0.00	$0.00	$0.00	$0.00	$405.00		$1,405.00
Total	$1,405.00	$0.00	$0.00	$0.00	$0.00	$405.00	$0.00	$1,405.00
West, Robert	This account needs to be reviewed. The payer may need to be called. Something is delaying payment.							
Patient	$0.00	$0.00	$0.00	$0.00	$0.00	$0.00		$0.00
Insurance	$0.00	$2,125.00	$0.00	$0.00	$0.00	$2,125.00		$2,125.00
Total	$0.00	$2,125.00	$0.00	$0.00	$0.00	$2,125.00	$0.00	$2,125.00
Still, Andrew	This account needs to be actively pursued. It should have been resubmitted or appealed by now.							
Patient	$0.00	$0.00	$0.00	$0.00	$0.00	$0.00		$0.00
Insurance	$0.00	$0.00	$2,125.00	$0.00	$0.00	$2,125.00		$2,125.00
Total	$0.00	$0.00	$2,125.00	$0.00	$0.00	$2,125.00	$0.00	$0.00
Steinberg, Marvin	This patient has been ignoring bills for too long. Call them, send to collections, or write-off the loss.							
Patient	$0.00	$0.00	$0.00	$500.00	$0.00	$500.00		$500.00
Insurance	$0.00	$0.00	$0.00	$0.00	$0.00	$0.00		$0.00
Total	$0.00	$0.00	$0.00	$500.00	$0.00	$500.00	$0.00	$500.00
Borish, Irvin	This account should be evaluated as a possible write-off.							
Patient	$85.00	$0.00	$0.00	$0.00	$85.00	$85.00		$85.00
Insurance	$0.00	$0.00	$0.00	$0.00	$0.00	$0.00		$0.00
Total	$85.00	$0.00	$0.00	$0.00	$85.00	$85.00	$0.00	$85.00
Ford, Loretta	This account should be reviewed. It appears to have been neglected by the biller, the payer, or both.							
Patient	$0.00	$0.00	$0.00	$0.00	$0.00	$0.00		$0.00
Insurance	$0.00	$0.00	$0.00	$0.00	$1,126.00	$1,126.00		$1,126.00
Total	$0.00	$0.00	$0.00	$0.00	$1,126.00	$1,126.00	$0.00	$1,126.00
Bunch, Cordia	Was this patient overcharged or did someone forget to enter a charge?							
Patient	$0.00	$0.00	$0.00	$0.00	$0.00	$0.00	$65.00	$65.00
Insurance	$0.00	$0.00	$0.00	$0.00	$0.00	$0.00		$0.00
Total	$0.00	$0.00	$0.00	$0.00	$0.00	$0.00	$65.00	($65.00)

(table continues)

TABLE 8. Accounts Receivable—Annotated *(continued)*

Patient Name	Current	30 Days	60 Days	90 Days	120 Days	Total	Unapplied	Net Total
Rorer, Sarah	A payment was received but not properly entered.							
Patient	$0.00	$0.00	$0.00	$0.00	$0.00	$0.00		$0.00
Insurance	$0.00	$0.00	$0.00	$0.00	$0.00	$0.00	$24.73	$24.73
Total	$0.00	$0.00	$0.00	$0.00	$0.00	$0.00	$24.73	($24.73)
Palmer, Daniel								
Patient	$0.00	$0.00	$1,500.00	$0.00	$0.00	$1,500.00		$1,500.00
Insurance	$0.00	$0.00	$0.00	$0.00	$0.00	$0.00		$0.00
Total	$0.00	$0.00	$1,500.00	$0.00	$0.00	$1,500.00	$0.00	$1,500.00
Bunch, Cordia								
Patient	$0.00	$0.00	$0.00	$0.00	$0.00	$0.00		$0.00
Insurance	$400.00	$0.00	$0.00	$0.00	$0.00	$400.00		$400.00
Total	$400.00	$0.00	$0.00	$0.00	$0.00	$400.00	$0.00	$400.00
Grand Total:								
Patient	$135.00	$0.00	$1,500.00	$500.00	$85.00	$2,135.00		$2,135.00
	6.32%	0.00%	70.26%	23.42%	3.98%	100.00%		100.00%
Insurance	$1,905.00	$2,225.00	$2,125.00	$100.00	$1,426.00	$6,781.00		$6,781.00
	28.09%	32.81%	31.34%	1.47%	21.03%	100.00%		100.00%
Total	$2,040.00	$2,225.00	$3,625.00	$600.00	$1,511.00	$8,916.00	$89.73	$8,826.27
	58.07%	13.46%	13.46%	4.49%	10.52%	100.00%		100.00%

Credit Balances

No matter how painstakingly a business tries to collect the correct amounts from patients, errors will inevitably be made. Some errors result in an overpayment, which is referred to as a "credit balance." The most efficient way to manage credit balances depends on the scope and type of practice. Large practices and practices where patients tend to be seen only occasionally may simply write a check and promptly return the money to the payer. Practices in which patients return for frequent follow-ups may offer the patient the choice between a refund or having the credit balance applied to a future amount due. Remember, the money belongs to the patient, not to your practice.

Sometimes a credit balance results from an overpayment from an insurance company. This can be due to an error on the insurance company's part, a reversal of the company's decision to pay a claim, or any of a number of other less-common circumstances. Regardless of how a credit balance comes to be, the overpayment should be promptly returned. This is not just a matter of business ethics; it also is a matter of financial efficiency. When an insurer does not receive a prompt refund, they often deduct the amount they believe to be due from future payments. This creates a bookkeeping nightmare, along with all the expenses that come with managing and cleaning up the resulting mess. In the case of Medicare, there are also legal and financial considerations. Medicare and some other payers charge interest on overpayments they make if the overpayments are not promptly refunded.

With this in mind, it is worth noting that Medicare and some other payers also pay interest to you when they are late in making payments. The definition of "late" varies with factors such as how the claim was submitted. Regardless how "late" is defined, the clock does not start until a clean claim is filed.

CASH OUTFLOW

Ultimately, monies that flow into your practice should flow out. There are several broad categories of outflows, including payroll. Payroll expenses include more than just salaries and wages; they include taxes and other costs associated with paying employees. Some portion of the revenues should be transferred from the business to the owners of the business as salary, bonus, or dividend.

Accounts Payable

Some of the revenues must be used to pay "fixed expenses." Fixed expenses are expenses to which you have previously committed, such as rent and insurance premiums. "Variable expenses" such as office supplies also draw money out of your practice's coffers. Together, fixed and variable expenses make up your Accounts Payable (A/P). Healthcare Entrepreneurs should think carefully before committing to fixed expenses and re-evaluate variable expenses to maximize profits.

As the name suggests, Accounts Payable (A/P) are the monies you should pay to others. In other words, an item on your A/P report belongs on another person or company's Accounts Receivable (A/R) report. A/P reports tend to be structured much like A/R reports, with columns showing when the bill is due and how long the bill has gone unpaid.

Many small and mid-sized businesses pay their bills before or when payment is due. Usually, this approach is good practice. Just as you appreciate prompt payment of monies due to you, your vendors and creditors appreciate receiving your payments in a timely manner. Moreover, by promptly paying your bills, you are improving your businesses' credit scores.

There are advantages to using a formal system to manage A/P, however. For example, A/P systems are helpful in cash flow forecasting as well as managing cash flow in general, and cash flow shortfalls, in particular. When viewed in the light of projected revenues, an A/P report helps warn when expenses may exceed revenues.

As Table 9 shows, most bills will appear in the "current" category. These are bills that are due on or soon after goods or services are received. Other bills are allowed to age for up to 30 days since the terms of the business agreement call for payment in 30 days or fewer. Few bills should go unpaid for more than 30 days. There are exceptions, however. For example, one bill from Computer Consultants, Inc., has been allowed to remain unpaid because the vendor sends out weekly invoices even when the amount due is the result of a portion of a job that is not yet completed. Similarly, the A/P report shows $2,175 unpaid for at least three months because there is a dispute over the bill. The disputed bill should be entered into the accounting system so that it is taken into account as part of the cash flow and does not fall through the cracks.

TABLE 9. Accounts Payable

	Current	1 - 30	31 - 60	61 - 90	> 90	TOTAL
AAA Medical Supplies	$ (997.13)	$ -	$ -	$ -	$ -	$ (997.13)
Behavioral Health Management Consultants	$(1,800.00)					
Blue Cross/Blue Shield	$ (75.28)	$ -	$ -	$ -	$ -	$ (75.28)
Computer Consultants, Inc.	$ (275.00)	$(221.00)	$(35.14)		$ -	$ (531.14)
County Utilities Department	$ (275.84)	$ -	$ -	$ -	$ -	$ (275.84)
Dubious Business Practices, Ltd	$ -	$ -	$ -	$ -	$(2,175.00)	$(2,175.00)
Home & Office Cleaners, LLC	$ -	$(350.00)	$ -	$ -	$ -	$ (350.00)
Lincoln Life, Administrative Agent	$ -	$(297.90)	$ -	$ -	$ -	$ (297.90)
Mary McMillan	$ (300.00)	$ -	$ -	$ -	$ -	$ (300.00)
TOTAL	**$(3,723.25)**	**$(868.90)**	**$(35.14)**	**$ -**	**$(2,175.00)**	**$(6,802.29)**

The A/P report also plays a role in loss prevention and budget management. When employees and others pay your bills, it is easy to lose sight of where revenues are being spent. A well-structured A/P system allows you to efficiently review bills and obligations before you authorize their payment. It also helps highlight expenses that are unnecessary or higher than necessary.

Paying Employees and Contractors

The considerations associated with paying employees and contractors are discussed at length in Chapter 6 and are not repeated here in-depth. Some points are worth reiterating, however. First, many Healthcare Entrepreneurs are employees of their own incorporated businesses. If that is the case, as an employee, you should pay yourself as regularly as you pay others. Your Accountant can best advise you how much salary you should receive to maintain your personal cash flow, maintain your corporate cash flow, and minimize income tax consequences. Expenses such as payroll taxes and fees paid to payroll services should be counted as payroll expenses. Payments to contractors are not payroll expenses.

PAYING YOURSELF

Among the advantages of owning your own business is an increased level of control over your own earnings. This does not mean complete control, but it does mean significantly enhanced control. Many variables underpin your ability to control your own income, including whether you are focused on the short-term or the long-term, and how willing you are to reinvest in your business.

Your practice is not a piggybank from which you can make withdrawals on a whim. Sometimes, withdrawals can be made with no real harm done to the company; however, sooner or later, ad-lib withdrawals may collide with some other force, such as a momentary lapse in cash flow, at which point the business can flounder and even fail. Monies should be withdrawn from your practice according to pre-determined schedules and criteria. Even when there are pressures to do otherwise, it is essential for the savvy Healthcare Entrepreneur to manage the temptation to plunder the practice.

There are many ways to remunerate yourself as a business owner. You can determine the best strategies with the help of Accountants and financial advisors. Since tax codes change, these strategies should be reviewed and, if appropriate, amended in the fall of each year.

Successful Healthcare Entrepreneurs almost always take some level of a fixed salary. There may be times, as in the opening months of practice, when there is barely enough income to pay the salary; nonetheless, you have worked for it, and you should take it. When there truly is not enough cash to cover your paycheck, the missed paycheck should be treated as a loan from you to the practice. A loan agreement should be recorded so that the practice can pay your salary when funds become available.

The precise amount of salary you take is best determined in consultation with financial advisers. Considerations such as payroll tax implications, the long-term impact on Social Security benefits, income tax rate, and a myriad of other factors influence the optimal base salary for each business owner.

The frequency with which you pay yourself also deserves some consideration. Most Healthcare Entrepreneurs have at least one employee in addition to themselves.

It makes sense to pay yourself on the same schedule that you pay clerical and other personnel.

Bonuses are another legitimate route for transferring money from the business into your personal accounts. By adding bonuses to your self-remuneration system, you allow yourself to maximize your earnings while leaving some degree of financial flexibility in the business. Bonuses are often tied to performance. In its general form, such a system involves paying yourself some portion of revenues earned when you meet or exceed a predetermined target. For example, if your expenses are in line with your budget and the actual revenues exceed the amounts you predicted by 20%, you can take the excess money as a bonus without harming your business.

Finally, owners of profitable businesses can receive dividends. If your business is incorporated, you are a stockholder in that corporation. If you are the sole owner, you own 100%of the stock. If you have three other partners, each holding an equal stake in the company, each of you owns 25% percent of the stock. Your stock, and the stock held by any partners, are like stocks traded over the counter by publicly traded companies. For example, your business can distribute profits by declaring dividends that are distributed in proportion to the distribution of the stocks. In other words, if one partner in a practice owns 60% of the stock and the other partner owns 40%, the amount determined as a dividend for a given period of time will be distributed on a 60:40 basis.

As a Healthcare Entrepreneur, you also may decide to reward yourself with one or more perquisites, commonly referred to as "perks." Many perks, such as automobiles, may be taxable by the IRS, so it is important to do the math to determine whether taking a perk works for or against the ultimate goal of maximizing personal income.

Initially, it may seem as though having the advantage of a tax-reducing expense for the practice automatically makes such perks a good idea. However, there are expense-side considerations as well. For example, a car that is considered a posses- sion of a business needs to be insured as a commercial vehicle and, as such, will be insured at a rate higher than the rate typically charged for a personal-use vehicle. Tax savings may be counterbalanced or completely offset by the cost of insurance. In addition, a vehicle that belongs to a practice must be used for business purposes only. You can track usage by keeping a log of any trips made for non-business pur- poses, but few among us are likely to make a note of every time we run out to the convenience store a mile away.

Another common perk is a retirement plan — a topic that is discussed in more depth in Chapter 10. Retirement plans range from an Individual Retirement Account (IRA) to more complex options such as a 401(k). The laws and regulations governing most of these plans are designed to prevent gross inequalities in how the plans benefit higher-paid versus lower-paid employees. Many plans require business owners to contribute to the retirement funds of their employees; yet, there is still room to set up retirement plans that are economically favorable for owners. Depending on how the plan is structured, a business owner may find that their personal wealth is enhanced even when the business bears the cost of funding the employee retirement plans. Secondary gains come in the form of employee loyalty and extended length of service.

Taxes, personal financial needs, and the practice's financial needs are among the considerations when deciding how to best compensate yourself. Salaries and bonuses will be taxed as regular income. Depending on how you structure the business and when you take the money, dividends may be taxed at a different rate.

Complicating matters just a bit are the ever-changing rules and ceilings associated with payroll taxes. Because these factors change, and because the equations can become complicated, use an Accountant to help determine how and how much each business owner is remunerated. An annual review of the compensation plan can be used to make adjustments in response to changes in tax rates and other fluctuating variables.

Dividends and Bonuses in Multi-Partner Groups

The distribution of dividends and bonuses becomes a bit more complex but still entirely manageable when there is more than one partner in a group. Bonuses can be, and typically are, tied to a performance measure or measures. Care must be taken to avoid setting up performance-based measures that may seem to serve as incentives for overutilization of services. Within that boundary, partners who bring more value to the business based on preset criteria can be awarded proportionally higher bonuses.

Distributions, on the other hand, must be divided equally across shares of stock. So, if two or more partners own equal amounts of stock but one of them significantly outperforms the others, there are no extra rewards for the higher-earning partner and no consequences for the partner who brought in less money. Fortunately, there are options with which to manage this situation.

Commonly, distributions are based on how much money remains at the end of a financial period, such as a fiscal year or quarter. Until the dividend amount is declared by the Board Of Directors, variables such as bonus amounts can be adjusted to make sure that any inequalities in the distribution at year's end have already been considered and counterbalanced. For example, a two-partner practice that awards bonuses in proportion to performance can distribute all profits as performance-based bonuses, thus avoiding conflicts involving dividends.

Laws And Government Relations

The term "government relations" is most commonly used to refer to political lobbying efforts. Here, the term is used to denote the fact that every Healthcare Entrepreneur has some relationship to a number of government agencies and entities at the federal, state, and local levels. Many of these entities have the power to promulgate laws, rules, and regulations that influence how you can practice clinically and how you operate your business. In practical terms, each relevant government agency is a partner who has some influence in your professional and business conduct. Therefore, it is essential for every Healthcare Entrepreneur to be familiar with and in compliance with the laws and regulations promulgated by those entities. Checklist 12 outlines units of the U.S. Department of Health and Human Services.

Disclaimer

The author is neither an Attorney nor a CPA, so nothing in this book should be construed as, let alone relied on, as legal or accounting advice. Competent legal counsel should be obtained whenever a matter of law is being considered. Competent accounting advice should be obtained whenever matters of taxation or

CHECKLIST 12

Units of the United States Department of Health and Human Services

✓ Administration on Aging

✓ Administration for Children and Families

✓ Agency for Healthcare Research and Quality

✓ Centers for Disease Control and Prevention

✓ Centers for Medicare and Medicaid Services

✓ Epidemic Intelligence Service

✓ Food and Drug Administration

✓ Health Resources and Services Administration

✓ Indian Health Service

✓ National Center for Health Statistics

✓ National Institutes of Health

✓ National Institute for Occupational Safety and Health

✓ Patient Affordable Healthcare Act Program

✓ Public Health Service & Office of the Surgeon General

✓ Substance Abuse and Mental Health Services Administration

[1]Each of these units has departments and other subdivisions.

accounting are being considered. This section is intended solely to orient you to a small sample of laws that govern healthcare practices. The sample includes laws governing business practices, employment, fraud and abuse, medical practice, collections, and privacy protection. By no means should this be regarded as an exhaustive list of relevant laws, nor should these brief synopses be regarded as thorough treatments of the laws and their implications.

PAYING TAXES

Income Taxes

Even solo practitioners have at least one business partner: Uncle Sam. The IRS, expects its share of your practice's income, just like any partner. The IRS also expects all sorts of documentation to ensure that you are operating your business in compliance with their rules. Depending on the legal jurisdiction in which you conduct business, you may have other taxing authorities to whom you also owe various duties, including filing tax forms and paying taxes.

Laws and regulations vary greatly from locale to locale. The IRS's requirements apply to us all. So, it is important to stay informed about state and local laws as well as IRS regulations. This section is focused primarily on the federal government of the United States of America.

To understand your obligations to the IRS, you must first know how your business is organized legally. The more common forms of business organization can be reviewed in Chapter 1. Healthcare Entrepreneurs who operate a practice that is incorporated, has employees, sponsors certain retirement plans, or subcontracts work to nonresident aliens must apply for and obtain a Taxpayer Identification Number (TIN), also known as an Employer Identification Number (EIN). This number identifies your business, and every tax-related thing you do, to the IRS. Applications for a TIN can be made by mail, fax, or online at https://sa.www4.irs.gov/modiein/individual/index.jsp.

The IRS defines a Sole Proprietor as "someone who owns an unincorporated business by himself or herself." If you are operating in this manner and meet other criteria, such as not having employees, your business can directly report its income tax obligations through your personal tax form (i.e., IRS Form 1040).

More commonly, practices are incorporated in other ways. Corporations such as single-member LLCs and others that have formally declared themselves to the IRS to be so-called S-Corps may report business taxes via the owner's personal tax report; however, most incorporated businesses must also file IRS Form 1120. Form 1120 is the business equivalent of your personal tax Form 1040 and is the form you use to declare your businesses' taxable income and deductions.

Payroll Taxes

In addition to the taxes on revenues, the IRS collects a cluster of taxes known collectively as "payroll taxes." In practical terms, every employer fills the role of a tax collector in that taxes are collected by the employers and then transmitted to the IRS. Payroll taxes include deductions taken from each owner's and employee's paycheck to cover their personal income tax obligations, amounts paid to the Social Security system, amounts paid to the Medicare fund, and amounts paid to the Federal Unemployment Trust.

> **TIP:** Calculating and paying payroll taxes is a time-consuming function that may be best outsourced to a payroll processing company.

Employers are charged with withholding estimated income taxes from their own paychecks and from each employee's paycheck every time a paycheck is issued. The same holds true when bonuses are paid. The amounts to be withheld are determined by consulting tax tables that change annually and are readily available from the IRS, on the internet, or through updates to computerized payroll systems.

Where each employee falls on the tax table is determined in part by the number of income tax allowances or deductions the employee wants to take advantage of. The declaration is made using IRS Form W4, the Employee's Withholding Allowance Certificate. No employee should receive a paycheck until they have provided a signed Form W4. Employees may change their declaration by submitting a new Form W4.

Other factors also help determine the amount of income tax withheld, such as whether the employee will be filing their personal income taxes as a married person, as a single person, or some other status. When employees change their marital status, the helpful Healthcare Entrepreneur, knowing that many employees do not think about such things, reminds the employee that they might want to consider revising their form W4.

Medicare taxes and Social Security taxes are collectively referred to as FICA withholding or simply FICA. FICA is the acronym for the Federal Insurance Contributions Act, which authorizes these taxes. The amounts of each tax are based on a percentage of each employee's income. The precise percentages change from time to time. After an employee's income reaches a specified ceiling, which also changes occasionally, the employer must stop withholding these taxes.

Employers are responsible for paying half of each employee's FICA, so when transmitting payroll taxes to the IRS, each employer transmits the sum of the amounts they have withheld from their employees, including FICA plus an employer's contribution, which is the equivalent to the amount of FICA withholdings. The actual report of these payments is made quarterly using IRS Form 941, the Employer's Quarterly Federal Tax Return.

When owners are not employees of their business or their business is not incorporated, the owner must pay Self-Employment Compensation Taxes (SECA). The amounts withheld for SECA are the same as those withheld from any employee; however, a key difference is that while companies pay half of FICA for employees, owners must pay all the required SECA taxes. To avoid a large end-of-the-year tax bill, many owners make SECA payments on a quarterly or more frequent scheduling. Self-employment compensation taxes are reported along with the owner's IRS form 1040 on IRS Schedule SE.

The Federal Unemployment Tax (FUTA) is a payroll tax that also is based on a percentage of payroll, which varies occasionally. FUTA is paid solely by the employer with no deductions taken from any employee's earnings. Small practices may pay

FUTA annually if their total FUTA obligation falls below a specified threshold; otherwise, FUTA must be paid quarterly. FUTA is reported annually using IRS form 940, The Employer's Annual Federal Unemployment (FUTA) Tax Return.

> **TIP:** Don't forget that many states and some local governments have taxes that must be paid by businesses operating in that jurisdiction.

Depending on the jurisdiction, other payroll taxes may also be required. Frequent examples include taxes to fund unemployment insurance (also called "re-employment insurance") or worker's compensation disability systems at the state level. The precise amounts of these taxes can and do change, so it is important to keep current on how much payroll tax to withhold and how much to pay. Penalties for late payments can be steep, so make each payment on time

Transmitting Taxes

There are several methods by which to pay taxes. One option is to file IRS forms and make federal tax payments electronically using the Electronic Federal Tax Payment System (EFTPS). Once you are established as an EFTPS user, you can file most of your business-related taxes online or via telephone, saving some of the time and clutter associated with paper forms. To enroll or learn more, go to www. irs.gov and enter "EFTPS enrollment" in the search box. Before you enroll, realize that once you start to file electronically, you cannot go back to paper.

TYPES OF LAWS

There is an old adage, often attributed to Abraham Lincoln, that says, "He who represents himself has a fool for a client." As a Healthcare Entrepreneur, your areas of expertise are your healthcare discipline and business, not law. Nonetheless, a basic familiarity with legal doctrines and terminology can help you develop sound policies and avoid pitfalls. Moreover, like it or not, some involvement with the law is inevitable when you practice any healthcare profession. For example, you will likely receive a subpoena for records at some time during your career.

What follows is a sampling of legal terms, legal concepts, and some federal laws that you may encounter in the course of your career. The goal is to provide a basic overview of selected points, not to make you a legal scholar. Therefore, just as a tour guide skims lightly over selected sites, each of which could be the subject of a day's viewing, this section provides a cursory view of subjects you may want to come back to in more depth if circumstances dictate doing so.

Statutory Law

When laypeople think of laws, they most often think in terms of statutory laws. Statutory laws are those made by a duly elected, duly empowered government body such as a legislature. However, there are other types of laws, including administrative laws, regulatory laws, and case law. Healthcare Entrepreneurs know the difference and use their knowledge to avoid legal problems and, sometimes, to capture legal advantages.

Regulatory Law

Many statutes include language that bestows on an unelected group or individual the authority to create and enforce rules and regulations. These rules and regulations constitute "regulatory law." Regulations carry the same weight, responsibilities, and consequences as the statute from which they were derived. Many of the common rights to due process that are carefully protected in the criminal justice system can be explicitly missing in cases involving regulatory law.

Two common and relevant examples of regulatory law include professional licensing laws and federal privacy laws such as HIPAA. At the federal level, broad sweeping powers are imparted through statutes such as HIPAA using language such as "The Secretary [of Health and Human Services] shall issue regulations. . . ." At the state level, your licensing law probably has few, if any, mandates or prohibitions that directly guide your conduct as a professional. Instead, most licensing laws create and empower a regulatory body whose rules you agree to follow when you accept a license to practice.

Ordained with broad authority, many licensing boards apply the principle of "community standard" to determine whether a licensee's conduct was acceptable. This can be an important factor when, for example, a practitioner engages in a behavior that is not explicitly prohibited or required but is generally seen as unacceptable or required under the community standard. In the event of a breach of a community standard, a professional may be penalized for actions or omissions for which they are not otherwise responsible. For that reason, wise Healthcare Entrepreneurs voluntarily hold themselves accountable to the dictates of ethics codes, practice standards, and other forms of credible professional guidance.

When a dispute involving regulatory law cannot be resolved, a case can be brought before an Administrative Law Judge (ALJ). For example, an ALJ may hear and decide about an argument made by a Healthcare Entrepreneur who believes that they were wrongly penalized by a federal payer following an audit.

Case Law

Case law is another form of law that can influence your practice. When a court or regulatory body makes a decision, that decision can influence decisions in future cases that are similar in nature. An example is the Tarasoff vs. Regents of the University of California decision by the California Supreme Court in 1974 and a revision by the same court in 1976. Simply put, the court ruled that mental health professionals who had knowledge of a threat to the safety of a potential victim had a duty to protect and warn that potential victim. From the moment that decision was made, mental health professionals practicing within the jurisdiction of that court had a duty to warn even though no statute or regulation in this regard had been created. Even though the duty to warn often conflicted with statutory or regulatory mandates for confidentiality, professionals around the nation began to practice as if they, too, held the duty to warn.

TIP: One way to help stay abreast of the glut of regulatory information pertaining to your field is to support and join your professional society and read its publications. Most such societies keep track of new laws and rules, and impending changes that will affect their members. You also can use internet tools to set up alerts that notify you when specific keywords are used online.

AN ANNOTATED GLOSSARY OF SOME LEGAL CONCEPTS AND TERMINOLOGY

Laypeople sometimes misunderstand medical terms and concepts. The same holds for legal terms and concepts. Both tend to have complex meanings, implications, and variants. The explanations offered here are presented in simple layman's terms that may not capture the full meaning of the term.

Arbitration is one of several methods of alternative dispute resolution. In arbitration, an Arbitrator, rather than a Judge, serves as the "Trier of Facts" and determines the disposition of the dispute.

Absolute liability refers to circumstances in which there are no mitigating factors to limit your liability.

Acquiescence is the abandonment of a right by not taking action to assert or preserve that right. Healthcare Entrepreneurs sometimes take a false sense of security from this concept, allowing themselves to assume that a patient who does not protest a procedure has, by dint of acquiescence, given consent. Savvy Healthcare Entrepreneurs do not settle for passive consent; instead, they talk to their patients, inform their patients, and evoke informed decisions from their patients.

Competence refers to the mental capacity of an individual to make informed decisions, participate meaningfully in contract negotiations or legal proceedings, and be held accountable for their actions. This is not as straightforward as it may seem because the term is used differently in various legal contexts. The granting of "informed consent" by a patient to a healthcare professional requires competence. For example, someone may argue that a patient who recently was diagnosed with a dementing illness may not be able to competently offer informed consent for subsequent treatment, diagnostic studies, or other interventions. It is important to remember that a person may be legally competent or legally not competent even when they are deemed incompetent by medical criteria. (See Checklist 4.)

Consideration is a term you may encounter when offering or agreeing to a contract. At the bottom line, something of value must be promised by each party to the other in order to make a contract binding.

Contracts of adhesion are also known as "leonine contracts" or "take it or leave it contracts." As the latter term suggests, these are contracts one party offers on a basis that leaves little or no ability for the receiving party to negotiate. Contracts from insurance companies and managed care organizations often are proffered as contracts of adhesion. Healthcare Entrepreneurs, nonetheless, make efforts to negotiate the terms to eliminate or reduce onerous requirements and to obtain more favorable terms.

Contributory negligence, in its basic form, allows for the assignment of some responsibility to an injured party, thus reducing the responsibility of the party who may have caused harm. Prudent Healthcare Entrepreneurs avoid taking comfort from this principle and instead take the lead and establish plans of care and after-care that are as error-proof as possible.

Damages are the monies paid to compensate a party for harm or losses incurred.

Default occurs when someone fails to take a required action in a civil matter. For example, if someone fails to appear for a hearing, the legal authority may deem that person to be in default and rule in favor of the other party. Healthcare Entrepreneurs never ignore legal documents or responsibilities, nor do they manage those without the advice and assistance of an Attorney.

Depositions are the pre-trial meetings in which both sides of a legal dispute interview a witness. The tone of a deposition can range from collegial to contentious. When a Healthcare Entrepreneur is being deposed, it is important to maintain a professional demeanor regardless of how others in the room comport themselves. When deposing an "expert witness" whose credible testimony is deleterious to their case, Attorneys are motivated to discredit the witness. Savvy Healthcare Entrepreneurs who are deposed as expert witnesses maintain their professional demeanor at all times.

Expert witnesses, as the name implies, are witnesses called to depositions, hearings, or trials to provide expert opinions to be considered. Different jurisdictions hold expert witnesses to different standards that govern how scientifically based their opinions must be. Expert witnesses are not responsible for making a case or advancing a legal argument — that is the job of the Attorneys. Instead, expert witnesses provide concise, defensible replies to the questions posed to them. They leave it to the Attorneys to ask additional questions before expounding on a topic. Expert witnesses usually can charge their typical reasonable fee for the time they spend preparing for and providing testimony.

Fact witnesses are witnesses called to depositions, hearings, or trials to testify about factual matters. For example, a fact witness may testify that their patient underwent a dental procedure on a specific date at a specific time. That same witness would not testify about the necessity or success of the procedure, since doing so would require expertise. Even when the witness has such expertise, it is not their responsibility to voice their opinions when serving as a fact witness. There also are potential liability issues that can emerge when a fact witness loses sight of their mission and offers expert opinions.

The distinction between a fact witness and an expert witness has business implications as well. In most jurisdictions, fact witnesses are paid a small sum to appear, while expert witnesses can charge their usual reasonable fee. Therefore, it is a good idea to have patients accept responsibility for paying for your time by including appropriate language in your Terms of Services Agreement.

Disciplinary hearings include hearings held by government agencies such as professional licensing boards to consider allegations made against a licensee. Often such boards have broad powers to impose penalties and sanctions, so it is never a good idea to attend a disciplinary hearing without a knowledgeable Attorney to represent you. Remember, even when the hearing is being conducted by colleagues, it can be a contentious, adversarial event.

Due process refers to the responsibilities and limitations imposed on authorities to ensure fairness and the enforcement of constitutional and other rights. Prudent Healthcare Entrepreneurs diligently take due process into account when dealing with employees who believe that their rights have been abridged.

Duty of care refers to the legal obligations to foresee and address possible harm to others by adhering to relevant standards of care.

Ignorantia juris non excusat is the Latin expression of the often spoken fact that "ignorance of the law is not a valid excuse" for breaching the law.

Legal Guardian is a status assigned and ordered by a court that allows the Guardian to manage the affairs of their ward. While other such arrangements can be made through agreements among individuals or entities, guardianship requires a court order. The distinction between a legal guardian and a "guardian in fact" is important. A guardian in fact is a person or entity who is performing the functions of a guardian without having been awarded the right to do so. Consider, for example, the parents of a developmentally impaired child who reached the age of majority. By continuing to care for every aspect of their child's needs, the parents have become their adult child's guardian in fact. But, until a court rules otherwise, they are not the legal guardians. So, for example, they may not have the authority to authorize a medical procedure until a court rules otherwise.

Negligence involves a breach of a legal duty, such as the duty of care.

Party refers to an individual or entity that enters into a contract or civil lawsuit.

Personal Representative is a HIPAA-specific term that refers to someone who has legal rights to act on behalf of the individual they represent when it comes to medical decision making. HIPAA specifies who "must" be regarded as a personal representative and who may not, despite all other appearances, be eligible to serve in that capacity.

Power of Attorney (POA) refers to the authorities imparted from one party to another, as proven by a legally sufficient document. POA documents may involve people, business entities, or both. There are several types of POAs, ranging from those that impart broad sweeping authority to those that are quite limited in their scope. Each type has its own unique terms and limitations, so these documents must be read carefully. Consider, for example, a POA that awards broad sweeping powers to make financial and end-of-life decisions but is silent on the subject of access to medical records.

Respondeat superior is the legal doctrine that supervisors can be held responsible for the acts of their employees or subordinates.

Standard of care is another term that has one meaning in the world of law and other meanings in other arenas. The level of caution a reasonable person would be expected to exercise is a key component of a standard of care.

> **TIP:** Subpoenas for records MAY NOT release you from responsibilities to maintain the confidentiality of your patient's medical records. Obtain a HIPAA-compliant release from your patient or consult with an Attorney before releasing protected patient information.

Subpoena is a document used to order someone to appear at a legal event such as a deposition, hearing, or trial. Although a subpoena may come from an Attorney without a judge's signature, a properly drafted and filed subpoena should be regarded as a court's order since the court can enforce it. It is not always the case that you have no other recourse when served with a subpoena; an Attorney can help you file motions to quash or limit the demands of a subpoena.

Subpoena duces tecum is a type of subpoena that requires someone to produce documents or materials. The subpoena often begins by demanding that the recipient bring specified documents or materials to a specific place at a specific time. Much of the time, the subpoena goes on to say that there is no need to appear personally if the documents or materials are received before the date of appearance. When that is not the case, it is worth contacting the Attorney to negotiate an agreement that the documents alone will satisfy the terms of the subpoena. Such an agreement should be followed by a written amendment to the subpoena and a written acknowledgment of receipt of the requested materials.

Trier of Fact and **Finder of Fact** refer to Judges, juries, Administrative Law Judges, Arbitrators, and others who are responsible for weighing evidence and making determinations in legal proceedings.

Torts occur when someone is harmed by the wrongful acts of another. Torts can and often do occur unintentionally, so before acting, prudent Healthcare Entrepreneurs think through their decisions, including the possibility of unintended consequences.

Vicarious liability refers to the legal responsibility imputed to one person or entity by means of their relationship to another.

Voir dire is the preliminary examination of a witness (or prospective juror) to establish or refute their eligibility to serve in that capacity. Since it is not uncommon for one side or both sides in a dispute to be unhappy with an expert witnesses' conclusions, the examination can sometimes feel assaultive. To exclude or diminish you as an expert witness, Attorneys may cast or imply aspersions on your training, methods, professionalism, and character. Healthcare Entrepreneurs maintain their professional demeanor, thus improving their chances of being "admitted as an expert" in the relevant jurisdiction.

LAWS ADDRESSING FRAUD AND ABUSE

The False Claims Act of 1863

The False Claims Act of 1863 (FCA) was written to address a tide of false claims made by defense contractors demanding payments from the government during the Civil War. In 1985, the False Claims Act was revamped and revitalized through a series of amendments. Still more amendments have been made in the 21st century. FCA and its amendments are now widely used to recoup payments made to those who provide goods and services in the healthcare industry. The wording of the FCA leaves room for even well-intentioned professionals and organizations to run afoul and be penalized.

Among the provisions of the law are provisions that encourage and reward unrelated parties, known as "whistleblowers," to bring possible FCA violations to light. Whistleblowers do not have to be directly involved with the reported offense. Labeled as "relators" rather than whistleblowers, those who report suspected violations are eligible to file "Qui Tam lawsuits." This serves to incentivize people to report possible FCA violations since a relator who wins such a suit can benefit financially. The Centers for Medicare & Medicaid Services (CMS) have actively encouraged such actions through campaigns asking beneficiaries to be on the alert for fraud and abuse.

Although there are other circumstances in which FCA may be called into play, these three are particularly relevant for Healthcare Entrepreneurs. In general, the FCA can be invoked when "any person who:

"(A) knowingly presents, or causes to be presented, a false or fraudulent claim for payment or approval (from a government entity");

"(B) knowingly makes, uses, or causes to be made or used, a false record or statement material to a false or fraudulent claim";

"(C) conspires to commit a violation of subparagraph (A), (B), (D), (E), (F), or (G)";

"(D) has possession, custody, or control of property or money used, or to be used, by the Government and knowingly delivers, or causes to be delivered, less than all of that money or property"; or

"(G) knowingly makes, uses, or causes to be made or used, a false record or statement material to an obligation to pay or transmit money or property to the Government, or knowingly conceals or knowingly and improperly avoids or decreases an obligation to pay or transmit money or property to the Government."

It is worth considering each of these prohibitions carefully because common sense interpretations do not always fit the reality of how they might be applied in court or in an administrative hearing.

For example, professionals often bill Medicare in good faith, applying their personal ethics to decisions regarding which procedures to render and which codes to use to bill for those procedures. However, Medicare has its own definitions of what constitutes a legitimate procedure and how each procedure should be coded.

Those definitions are embedded in countless pages dense with policies, procedures, coverage determinations, and advisories, each of which is subject to revision from time to time. It is up to the Healthcare Entrepreneur to know about and comply with the payer sources' definitions and policies.

Federal Anti-Kickback Statute

The Federal Anti-Kickback Statute is intended to prohibit the practice of paying for referrals to services for which a government entity might be called upon to pay. This is a criminal act with penalties for violations ranging up to five years. It also has provisions for steep monetary fines and provisions for civil penalties that can exceed three times the amount of any overpayment made by the government.

Unlike several related laws, the standard for prosecution under this act requires that the violation be "knowing and willful." Penalties for violations can be levied against both the payer and the recipient of a payment. At the bottom line, the financial consequences of anti-kickback violations can be staggering.

The statute does specify a number of "safe harbors" from which Healthcare Entrepreneurs can exchange things of value and make referrals to each other without running afoul of the law. For example, employees and owners of the same corporation can make referrals to each other without triggering the statutes. On the other side of the coin, the exchange of "anything of value" can be construed as a kickback. So, wise Healthcare Entrepreneurs consult with legal counsel before exchanging anything of value with a current or potential referral source.

Stark Laws

What is colloquially known as the Stark Laws, or simply Stark, is actually a series of laws, regulations and provisions embedded in larger bills such as the Balanced Budget Act of 1995 (BBA). Essentially, Stark is focused on limiting certain types of referrals to resources or entities in which the healthcare professional or a family member has a vested interest. Stark is a bit less toothy than some other referral control laws insofar as there are no criminal penalties prescribed in Stark. However, even unintentional violations of Stark can result in hefty financial penalties.

Stark pertains only to certain professions and certain medical businesses known as designated health services (DHSs). It applies when services are rendered to patients who are insured by certain government payers. In an abundance of caution, Healthcare Entrepreneurs who are covered by Stark may choose to forego permissible business and referral options to avoid the appearance of a breach of the law and to stay within the parameters of what has become a community standard. Since some related state laws are more encompassing and more restrictive than Stark, it is important to know the relevant laws in your state.

LAWS ADDRESSING HEALTHCARE DELIVERY

The Medicare Access and CHIP Reauthorization Act of 2015

The Medicare Access and CHIP Reauthorization Act of 2015 (MACRA) is the source of some of the most sweeping changes in the healthcare industry this century. This complex, nearly 2,400-page legislation touches on many aspects of healthcare. At its core, MACRA pushes aside the traditional system in which payment for healthcare services was based on considerations such as cost, time, and effort, and establishes "value-based payment" as the standard for healthcare services remuneration. While MACRA itself is focused on Medicare, the rest of the insurance industry and many healthcare professions have also been migrating toward the new system.

MACRA details two models of reimbursement. The first is the Merit-Based Incentive Payment System (MIPS). In this system, Healthcare Entrepreneurs and others are evaluated on four weighted criteria, including quality, interoperability, improvement, and cost. Quality is determined by the completion of performance measures developed by the payer and implemented by the healthcare professions.

Interoperability is sometimes referred to as Advancing Care Information (ACI). The interoperability criteria involve the secure use of Electronic Health Records features such as e-prescribing and reporting to public health agencies. Improvement can be demonstrated through activities such as completing various trainings or implementing programs of care coordination. The cost criteria include metrics such as Medicare Spending Per Beneficiary (MSPB) and other narrower financial data pertaining to various specialties.

Medicare providers are scored along these four dimensions. High scorers are rewarded with increased payment based on a percentage increase over the standard Medicare fee schedule. On the other hand, low scorers are penalized with reduced payments calculated by applying a percentage-based penalty to the standard fee schedule.

Another set of changes and programs codified in MACRA are the Advanced Alternative Payment Models (APMs). APMs allow Healthcare Entrepreneurs to earn incentive payments in exchange for accepting more risk, providing more cost-efficient care, and improving the quality of care. Unlike MIPS, where participation is mandatory for many healthcare professionals, including soloists, involvement in APMs is targeted toward larger organizations such as Accountable Care Organizations (ACO).

LAWS GOVERNING PATIENT RIGHTS

The Health Insurance Portability and Accountability Act of 1996

The Health Insurance Portability and Accountability Act of 1996 (HIPAA) significantly affects a broad range of healthcare practice and related functions. Sometimes referred to as the Kassebaum-Kennedy Act, this is a complex and often-misunderstood law that has an impact on virtually all healthcare professionals.

In theory, there should be some healthcare professionals who are not covered under HIPAA. In reality, virtually anyone who provides healthcare services, and certainly all Healthcare Entrepreneurs, meet the legal definition of a Covered Entity (CE) whose actions are controlled by HIPAA and the associated regulations.

The rules define CEs as (1) health plans, (2) healthcare clearinghouses, and (3) healthcare providers who electronically transmit any health information in connection with transactions for which the U.S. Department of Health and Human Services (HHS) has adopted standards.

HIPAA mandates that patients and customers be informed of their rights and each practice's policies pertaining to their rights. The duty to inform falls to the healthcare providers, who must give their patients and customers a privacy notice that meets specified criteria. This is accomplished by providing patients with a HIPAA-compliant Notice of Privacy Practices (NPP).

HIPAA and its associated rules fall into four broad categories, referred to as "standards." Perhaps best known is the Privacy Standard, which confers certain rights on patients and responsibilities on healthcare professionals. The Privacy Standard also includes rules designed to protect the confidentiality of specific healthcare-related data classified as Protected Health Information (PHI).

Among the rights conferred on patients is the right to view and obtain copies of their health records, determine to whom PHI can be released, and for what purpose. When PHI is released, patients have a right to know what was released, to whom, and how. So, CEs are advised to maintain an accurate log of all releases of PHI. Although patients have the right to obtain copies of the health records, ownership and responsibility for maintaining the record remain with the eligible profession or their appropriately designated medical records custodian.

The HIPAA Security Standards for the Protection of Electronic Protected Health Information address requirements for ensuring that certain healthcare information that is held or transmitted in electronic form be protected from loss. Conceptually, HIPAA bestows certain rights of access to their healthcare records on healthcare recipients; denial of such access is considered a civil rights violation. Accordingly, infractions and complaints are handled by the Office of Civil Rights (OCR) within HHS. CEs are therefore charged with protecting that information from a wide range of threats such as acts of nature like floods and criminal acts such as data theft. The cost of taking steps to comply with the security standards can be quite high, so options for compliance are scalable. Scalability means that acceptable efforts to comply with the standards differ from smaller to larger covered entities.

HIPAA's Identification Standard requires that all CEs register for numeric identifiers to be used in all HIPAA-related transactions. For Healthcare Entrepreneurs, the numeric identifier is their National Provider Identifier (NPI) number. This is a unique, 10-digit identification number for which each Healthcare Entrepreneur must apply. To obtain an NPI, you must register at https://nppes.cms.hhs.gov/NPPES/Welcome.do.

The HIPAA Transaction Standards are also known as the Administrative Simplification Standards. These standards are supposed to guide the establishment of uniform standards, operating rules, and coding for the management and transmission of information covered by HIPAA.

As is often the case with laws touted as "healthcare reform," the advantages of these standards fall largely to third-party payers. Therefore, when it comes to compliance, most of the heavy lifting falls to the payers and to support companies such as the software companies that sell medical billing software. Small business owners and professionals should nonetheless be familiar enough with these standards to ensure that the products and services they purchase or lease are compliant.

> **TIP:** Many federal laws have counterpart laws at the state level. The federal and state-level laws governing the same topic may not always jive. As a rule of thumb, federal law trumps state law. BUT, THERE ARE EXCEPTIONS! You should be aware of relevant laws at both levels of government.

See Checklist 13 for important details about HIPAA compliance.

The 21st Century Cures Act (PL 114-255)

The 21st Century Cures Act was intended to promote research and innovation in healthcare. A portion of the Act focused on Electronic Health Records and interoperability. Rules have been promulgated under the act which mandate that patients have easy and speedy access to their medical records. Of particular note is the requirement that, with some exceptions, each of eight types of clinical documents must be made available to patients and others without delay (see Checklist 14).

CHECKLIST 13

HIPAA Compliance: Things to Remember

✓ Purchase a HIPAA compliance manual.

✓ Send your compliance officer for formal training, either online or in person.

✓ Conduct and update your security risk assessment as required by the security rules. There are tools and guidance at www.CMS.gov.

✓ Develop and put into use your privacy notice.

✓ Train ALL of your staff –no exceptions.

✓ Obtain Business Associates Agreements as needed.

✓ Implement and enforce all of the policies in your HIPAA compliance manual.

✓ Monitor compliance on a routine basis. When there is a breach or violation, add tracking of the policies underlying the breach to your routine monitoring.

✓ Respond immediately to any suspected breach. Nothing is too insignificant. Willful neglect may be construed as an infraction in and of itself.

- Take immediate action to mitigate any possible breach.
- Investigate the root causes, documenting the investigation as you go.
- Develop and implement solutions with input from staff. Don't forget to reflect the changes in updates to your compliance manual.
  - Time is of the essence, so take immediate action.
  - In addition to modifying policies and procedures, it may be necessary to repeat training, take disciplinary actions, and alter equipment.

✓ Although technically you do not have to report every untoward event, there are reporting requirements which, if ignored, can make a bad situation worse. Report breaches in a timely manner.

CHECKLIST 14

Documents Covered By the 21st Century Cares Act

✓ Consultation notes

✓ Discharge summary notes

✓ History and physical

✓ Imaging narratives

✓ Laboratory report narratives

✓ Pathology report narratives

✓ Procedure notes

✓ Progress notes

Many EHR programs allow clinicians to designate which documents will be made available to patients on their portal. The same law provides penalties for Clinicians who engage in "information blocking" which, in general, means failing to make all non-exempt portions of each patient's record available to the patient without delay.

The Health Information Technology for Economic and Clinical Health Act of 2009

The Health Information Technology for Economic and Clinical Health Act (HITECH) was signed into law as part of the American Recovery and Reinvestment Act (ARRA) of 2009. The fact that HITECH was embedded in ARRA is noteworthy in that it provides a lesson for Healthcare Entrepreneurs. Specifically, laws that have profound impacts on your business may be embedded, and to that extent hidden, in laws that seem unrelated and to which you might not pay any attention.

HITECH, like HIPAA, is also broad ranging, with extensive, sometimes complex requirements. It was intended to encourage the adoption of Electronic Health Records while strengthening the privacy and security standards of those records. Since both acts deal with patient records, they intertwine. For example, while HIPAA addresses the release of protected health information, HITECH prescribes a minimum necessary standard limiting information releases to just the information needed to accomplish the purpose of the release.

> **TIP:** Despite popular belief, there is no single fee for releasing healthcare records; the appropriate fee to charge for copying and providing records varies with the circumstance. With some exceptions, Healthcare Entrepreneurs establish their own fee structure for this service and modify that structure to fit each unique circumstance.

Another HITECH requirement that impacts many practices is the granting of a patient's right to receive copies of their records electronically under certain circumstances. Fees for providing electronic records are limited.

HITECH defines "data breach" as "the unauthorized acquisition, access, use or disclosure of Protected Health Information which compromises the security or privacy of such information, except where the unauthorized person to whom such information is disclosed would not reasonably have been able to retain such information."

One easily overlooked source of a data breach so defined can occur if a Business Associate accesses protected information without a Business Associate's Agreement in place. HITECH extended the concept of Business Associates to include all those who have access to protected health information, including businesses and individuals who do not meet the definition of a covered entity.

HITECH created tougher, more burdensome responsibilities for tracking and reporting data breaches. Specifically, a log of all data security breaches must be maintained and submitted annually to HHS. If a breach involves more than 50 people, the local news media must be notified so they can help spread the word about the breach. Regardless of the size of the breach, those whose information has been breached must be notified individually by mail within 60 days. When breaches involve a Business Associate, the Business Associate must notify the covered entity, which then must take the appropriate actions. Under-reacting can be costly, bringing the risk of fines as high as $1.5 million per violation.

Another aspect of HITECH that every Healthcare Entrepreneur should keep in mind when making policies has to do with who might benefit from a breach and who is culpable in the event of a breach. Identified as "victims," patients themselves may reap the reward of a portion of any fines levied. Similarly, state-level Attorneys General can file civil lawsuits in the event of a HITECH violation. In practical terms, the traditional Healthcare Entrepreneur-patient relationship has been altered, and not for the better. Defensive healthcare practices are regrettably necessary to counterbalance the changes.

A Cautionary Note About Releasing Healthcare Records
Requests for copies of healthcare records can come from any of a variety of sources. Laws governing your response to these requests can vary from jurisdiction to jurisdiction. Complicating matters, laws governing the release of records can be contradictory. For example, in some jurisdictions, whoever pays for a procedure is entitled to the record pertaining to that procedure. This can get dicey when, for example, the parent of a minor child pays for their child's treatment and then, after the child reaches the age of majority, demands a copy of the record despite their now-adult offspring's objections. Releasing the record in this situation may violate the patient's privacy rights, while failing to release may violate the payer's rights to access.

Certainly, each patient has a right to obtain copies of their own records. Patients also have the right to authorize others to obtain their records. This, too, can be problematic. For example, patients often unwittingly authorize their insurance companies to have unrestricted access to their medical records when they purchase an insurance policy. This allows insurance companies to request some or all of a patient's record.

Attorneys representing your patient or opposing your patient in a legal matter may also subpoena healthcare records. People who have or claim to have Power of Attorney (POA) also request records. The list goes on. Unfortunately, a subpoena is not always appropriately filed, a POA may not cover health records, and other claims of authority are simply overstated. The burden is on you to be sure the person to whom you release protected information is, in fact, entitled to such information without putting you in a legally precarious position. Policies and procedures guiding the release of healthcare records in general, and protected information in particular, are an essential tool in preventing errors and reducing liability involving breaches of confidentiality.

The Fair Debt Collection Practices Act of 1977

The Fair Debt Collection Practices Act of 1977 (FDCPA) and subsequent amendments are administered by the Federal Trade Commission (FTC). The FDCPA guides the practices of those attempting to collect a debt. Consequences for violations of what the act refers to as "abusive and deceptive" practices include regulatory actions by the FTC and possible civil actions by the debtor.

The FDCPA places much responsibility on debt collectors, including their office staff, who are attempting to collect payment on a past-due bill. Staff members charged with contacting patients and others regarding past-due bills should be trained and held responsible for taking certain required actions and avoiding saying or doing things that might infringe on the debtor's rights.

The person contacting the debtor via phone or written correspondence must identify themselves as a debt collector. Calls and correspondence should also begin with an advisory to the debtor that any information obtained will be used to affect the collection of the debt. Debtors must also be advised of their right to dispute the debt.

As a creditor attempting to collect the debt, you must provide verification of the debt to any consumer who requests in writing that you do so. Failure to respond to such a consumer request is tantamount to writing off the debt because all collections efforts must cease unless and until the request for verification is appropriately addressed. If collection efforts advance to the point of legal actions and lawsuits, the FDCPA includes rules guiding those actions.

There are several prohibitions associated with debt collection that can be summarized and stated in a positive light for ease of staff training. For example, contacts with debtors must be conducted during reasonable hours in a respectful, honest, non-abusive manner. If a debtor indicates that calls to the debtor's place of work are unacceptable, such calls should cease. Harassing and embarrassing actions must also be avoided.

> **TIP:** Before outsourcing collections activities, make sure the collections agent you retain is knowledgeable about and compliant with all state and federal laws as well as your profession's ethical standards.

The Controlling the Assault of Nonsolicited Pornography and Marketing Act of 2003 (CAN-SPAM)

Messages that are "primarily commercial" in content are covered by the Controlling the Assault of Nonsolicited Pornography and Marketing Act of 2003 (CAN-SPAM) and associated regulations. The Federal Trade Commission (FTC) is responsible for implementing and enforcing this law. Penalties for infractions are steep. Despite the implications of the act's name, emails and other electronic communications do not have to be mass distributed to fall under the purview of CAN-SPAM.

A message is deemed to be "primarily commercial" when it advertises or promotes a commercial product or service. In contrast, messages that facilitate a previously agreed-upon transaction that provides an existing customer with information about an ongoing business transaction is classified as a "transactional" or "relationship" communication. Transactional communications are less heavily regulated than "primarily commercial" communications.

As email and other forms of mass marketing proliferate, the savvy Healthcare Entrepreneurs must consider how blurry the legally defined lines can be. This is particularly true if untrained or undertrained staff members are charged with developing or implementing a marketing campaign. Consider, for example, a Dermatologist who emails a promotional offer for cosmetic Botox to all of the patients on their existing patient list. Can the patients who previously transferred their care to another Dermatologist still be considered existing customers, or must their names be deleted from the list? Can patients who have only been treated for medical conditions and have never purchased cosmetic services or products be regarded as existing customers when the Dermatologist is marketing just cosmetic products? In addition to addressing these concerns, the dermatology practice should consider its obligations under HIPAA before embarking on such a campaign.

Prudent Healthcare Entrepreneurs may err on the side of caution by treating all mass communications as primarily commercial. Using this strategy, the Healthcare Entrepreneur would first confirm that targeted recipients of a mass communication have previously agreed to receive such communications, then also ensure that the communication:

1. Does not include false or misleading information in the subject line or header.
2. Does identify the practice and includes accurate information regarding the sender, the recipient, and the originating domain name.
3. Does specifically identify the message as an advertisement.
4. Does provide recipients a valid postal address to which they can communicate.

5. Does clearly and conspicuously advise recipients how to opt-out of receiving future communications. Opt-out requests should be fulfilled within 10 days and without consequence to the recipient.

BUSINESS LAWS

The Sherman Antitrust Act

The Sherman Antitrust Act of 1890 (Sherman Act) states that "Every contract, combination in the form of trust or otherwise, or conspiracy, in restraint of trade or commerce among the several States, or with foreign nations, is declared to be illegal." At the bottom line, the Sherman Act and other antitrust laws were written to restrain business practices that are believed to be anticompetitive.

The Clayton Antitrust Act

The Clayton Antitrust Act of 1914 (Clayton Act) expanded the implications and reach of the Sherman Act. Under the Clayton Act, the right to sue was expanded to empower "any person who shall be injured in his business or property by reason of anything forbidden in the antitrust laws."

Even though these acts were originally intended to apply to large monopolies, their prohibitions now also apply to small businesses, including healthcare practices.

These two laws, and others that are related, can be complex and marked by thin lines. For example, Healthcare Entrepreneurs who share pricing information may be accused of antitrust activities. At the same time, in many states, insurance companies are required to post their fees and terms so that each company knows where their competitors stand. Therefore, the savvy Healthcare Entrepreneur treads carefully in this arena and seeks appropriate legal counsel when working with others, be they competitors or partners in joint ventures.

Potentially Monopolistic or Anticompetitive Practices

Some of the things to watch for while working with others are listed below. All actions listed are not necessarily illegal; nor are actions that are not listed necessarily permitted. As always, the prudent Healthcare Entrepreneur consults with a competent Attorney when faced with matters of law.

1. Price fixing
2. Agreements not to compete with a competitor
3. Agreements to restrict production or output
4. Agreements to restrict certain business activities
5. Boycotts

6. Professional codes of ethics that unreasonably restrict how professionals compete
7. Tying access to one product to the condition that a consumer purchase a second product
8. Creating a monopoly in an anticompetitive manner
9. Predatory pricing

LABOR AND EMPLOYMENT LAWS

The Fair Labor Standards Act

The Fair Labor Standards Act of 1938 (FLSA) addresses issues such as minimum wages, overtime pay, recordkeeping, and child labor. FLSA is meant to apply only to enterprises engaged in interstate commerce with $500,000 in the annual dollar volume of business. It is included here because it also applies to various populations (such as the disabled) and settings (such as schools) to whom and in which professionals sometimes render services.

> **TIP:** Several states have set minimum wages above the federal minimum wage level. Know and comply with your state's laws.

Given the proliferation of multisite practices, partnerships, mergers, and joint ventures, some awareness of FLSA is warranted whenever a practice plans an expansion. Employers who are subject to the FLSA's minimum wage provisions must post a notice explaining the Act in a conspicuous place in each of their locations.

The Occupational Safety and Health Act of 1970

The Occupational Safety and Health Act of 1970 (OSHA) defines an employer as any "person engaged in a business affecting commerce who has employees" except specific government entities. OSHA is administered by the U.S. Department of Labor (DoL), which promulgates wide-sweeping rules and standards. Information, materials, and guidance to promote compliance are available at www.OSHA.gov.

> **TIP:** All covered employers are required to display the OSHA "Job Safety and Health: It's the Law" poster unless the employer's workplace is located in a state that operates an OSHA-approved state plan.

Under OSHA, it is the duty of the employer to provide "a place of employment which is free from recognized hazards that are causing or are likely to cause death or serious physical harm to his employees." Employers, including those in healthcare, must comply with the standards promulgated by OSHA.

Many professionals fail to recognize the hazards that are inherent in their work or the in the work of their employees. So, a thorough risk assessment is in order. A number of safety issues are common in healthcare settings, such as access to viable emergency exits, code-compliant electric wiring, and protection from common toxic substances such as cleaning solutions. Still other OSHA-regulated issues come into play in specialty offices where radiation, flammable gases, or biohazards are present. Even if you do not have any employees, compliance with OSHA standards is good risk-management practice.

The Employee Retirement Income Security Act of 1974

The Employee Retirement Income Security Act of 1974 (ERISA) is administered by the Employee Benefits Security Administration (EBSA), a branch of the U.S. Department of Labor (DoL). Title I of ERISA addresses employee rights and, therefore, employer responsibilities in the arena of retirement plans. If you, as an employer, offer retirement or health insurance benefits to yourself or your employees, you likely are covered by ERISA.

ERISA is a complex bill that covers a lot of ground. It is filled with responsibilities for employers, some of which would surprise the average person. Penalties for violations of ERISA are steep. They include potentially large fines and the possibility of jail time. Professional Plan Administrators should be retained to ensure compliance. Likewise, perks such as employee health insurance should be purchased through an insurance broker whose services include keeping their clients in compliance with ERISA requirements.

Remember, even if you retain a professional Plan Administrator and other advisors, you still have fiduciary responsibilities. As always, consult an Attorney and other relevant professionals before you enter the arena of employee benefits and retirement plans.

The Americans with Disabilities Act

Written and enforced as a civil rights act, the Americans with Disabilities Act (ADA) is intended to protect the rights of people who have disabilities. ADA was amended by The Americans with Disabilities Act Amendments Act of 2008 (ADAAA). Both are regulated and enforced by the U.S. Equal Opportunity Commission. The act has five subsections, called "titles." Title I addresses discrimination in the workplace.

ADA is a complex law laden with legally binding terms that do not always match the definitions used in daily parlance and are subject to interpretation on a case-by-case basis. For example, employers who are covered by ADA must provide "reasonable accommodations" for "qualified" applicants and employees provided the accommodations do not impose an "undue hardship" on the employer.

The goal of the act is to ensure applicants and employees are not blockaded from employment if they could perform the essential functions of a job if accommodations were made for their disability. Compliance with ADA starts before employment begins. For example, there are realms of questioning an employer may not pursue in an interview.

ADA applies to companies with 15 or more employees; however, the principles of ADA are widely accepted and in many locales form the community's standards. So, the prudent Healthcare Entrepreneur complies with ADA even when they have fewer than 15 employees.

> **TIP:** Several laws have trigger points, defined by the number of employees, beyond which employers have new and increased responsibilities and obligations.

Whistleblower Protections

As many as 16 federal labor laws have so-called whistleblower protections. In a nutshell, employees covered by whistleblower protections may file complaints if they believe that they have experienced discrimination or retaliation for exercising any of the rights afforded by the relevant law. Successful complaints can serve as a prelude to other legal actions that the prudent employer would seek to prevent and avoid.

Savvy Healthcare Entrepreneurs offer employees safe and ample opportunities to express their ideas and concerns directly to the Healthcare Entrepreneur. In general, Healthcare Entrepreneurs create an office culture in which everyone accepts responsibility for proactively expressing concerns and pointing out violations of laws, rules, contracts, and ethics as soon as any concern occurs to them.

Retirement And Long-Range Planning

Starting a new business is exciting and inherently rewarding. Perhaps that is why it is so easy to get immersed in the details of the start-up. However, part of starting a business involves long-term planning as well as organizing the first few steps. How you envision the far end of your career as a Healthcare Entrepreneur will influence how you manage the middle years and your retirement.

RETIREMENT PLANNING

Building a business that has a saleable value is part of the Healthcare Entrepreneur's credo. For most Healthcare Entrepreneurs, the proceeds from selling their practice, or their share of a practice, constitute a sizeable portion of their financial net worth and retirement portfolio. However, it is seldom wise to put all of one's investment eggs in a single basket. So, in addition to investing in their practices, Healthcare Entrepreneurs also begin funding other investments and retirement plans from the earliest days of their career.

The term "retirement plan" has multiple meanings. It can describe your fantasies of cruising the world or fishing on a crystal-clear lake. It can also refer to the budgets and projections you make when you are trying to estimate how much savings you will need to retire comfortably. In this chapter, the term is used to refer to pension plans and similar structures that allow you to save money, most often with a tax advantage.

Retirement plans are a must for prudent Healthcare Entrepreneurs. The earlier you begin saving for retirement, the better. Far too often, professionals get to the point where they want to, or must, retire but are financially unable to do so without a significant decline in their lifestyle. All things being equal, an investor who makes consistent monthly contributions to their retirement investment accounts beginning when they are 30 years old will have almost three times the amount to use in retirement than the investor who waits to start investing until they are 40 years old.

As a business owner, you are in a better position than most to choose the type of retirement instruments in which you wish to invest. You can also choose what types of retirement plans your business sponsors. There is no "best plan" for everyone.

Individual Retirement Plans

One popular form of pension plan is the traditional Individual Retirement Plan (IRA). IRAs come in two basic forms: traditional IRAs and Roth IRAs. Traditional IRAs allow for investment contributions up to a ceiling that has been determined by statute. They can be set up easily through almost any investment house and most banks. The amount you can contribute to a traditional IRA is tax-deductible at the time the contribution is made. Later, when you retire and begin to withdraw funds from the IRA, the amounts you withdraw will be taxed.

In contrast, the money you contribute to a Roth IRA is taxed when you earn it, but the subsequent withdrawals of that money are tax-free. In both cases, there are contingencies for early withdrawal for specific purposes, such as education and health. Withdrawing money from an IRA before reaching pre-defined retirement criteria can lead to hefty financial consequences.

Simplified Employee Pension IRA

A Simplified Employee Pension IRA (SEP) is a pension plan that is available to employers and sole proprietors. The primary advantage of a SEP over other IRAs is that SEPs allow for higher contribution amounts than the others. On the other side of the coin, SEPs are employer-sponsored plans. The contributions to each employee must be equal. So, if you contribute 10% of your income to your SEP, you must also contribute 10% to every other participant's account. Employees remain in control over how their money is invested with the parameters of the plan document on file with the Internal Revenue Service (IRS).

TIP: Pre-tax money is earned income that is sheltered from immediate taxation when it is invested in certain pension plans, and vehicles such as medical saving accounts. Although there are exceptions to the rule, in general it is a good idea to take advantage of programs that have pre-tax protections as a feature.

401(k) Plans

401(k) plans typically have higher contribution ceilings than traditional and Roth IRAs. They also allow you to save higher amounts of tax-deductible monies. 401(k)s also require that all employees be eligible for and receive contributions from the company that sponsors the plan.

401(k)s are, in some ways, a bit complex. They require the filing of copious documents with the IRS. These documents serve, among other things, to ensure that all employees' rights are being protected. Accordingly, there are start-up costs for plan administrators who draw up the documents and ensure that the plan complies with all laws and regulations. Plan Administrators help determine the right balance between company contributions to employees and employer's financial benefits. Remember, the contribution to employees is not just an expense to the company; it is often an incentive for an employee to remain at the company.

TRANSITION AND EXIT PLANNING

Business experts invariably recommend that every business plan includes exit strategies and plans for the transition of ownership and leadership that ensure the business continues and the profit potentials are realized. Although these plans will change over time as the business or other circumstances change, exit planning should be a part of every start-up plan.

When more than one person owns a practice, their partnership agreements should provide predetermined routes of transition and exit. Although there are many variations on the theme, it is important for partnership documents to specify the terms by which stock can be transferred or sold by a partner who wants to leave the practice. Perhaps because decisions of this sort are inherently complex, the contractual language surrounding these options also tends to be complex.

Here is just one example of how such language might be constructed. The partners who are remaining have the "first right of refusal" to purchase the stock of the partner who is leaving. This means that the partners who plan to remain may purchase the departing partner's shares at a predetermined price. The price can be expressed in dollars or in a formula that varies with a factor such as last year's revenues.

Should the remaining partners decline to exercise this option, the departing partner may present a viable buyer to the remaining partners for their consideration. The viable buyer must meet all the requirements previously specified in the partnership agreements. The remaining doctors can either accept the proposed buyer or cast a veto. To prevent the veto from being abused, it can only be used a predetermined number of times, after which the departing partner can sell their interests without input from the remaining partners.

Looking beyond the terms of partnership agreements, there are several key ingredients in a viable exit and transition plan. Some of these ingredients require estimates and assumptions, such as how long you will remain healthy enough to practice. Unexpected life events aside, start with your best estimate as to when you want to leave your practice. This can be determined in terms of age, personal net worth, the sale value of the practice, or any other determinant you choose. Remember, sales seldom happen overnight, so you likely will need to begin seeking buyers and start transitions well before you reach your target.

Another ingredient in exit planning involves determining how you will exit. As a Healthcare Entrepreneur, you retain the right to simply shutter your business and walk away (after attending to financial obligations and the continuity of care for your patients). However, this is not really a Healthcare Entrepreneurial option. As a Healthcare Entrepreneur, you have built a saleable business, the benefits of which should be reaped. At the bottom line, a Healthcare Entrepreneurial exit plan always ends with a sale. A well-formed exit plan includes the pros, cons, and strategies associated with each of the types of buyers you imagine your business might attract. For example, planning to sell to a junior associate requires different strategies than planning to sell to a buyer you just met.

There is much that needs to be transferred when a professional departs from a practice. Responsibility for patients tops the list. As a Healthcare Entrepreneur, you also have a corpus of knowledge and experience that should be passed on to whoever takes your place. This includes your business's unique features, leadership skills, and, in many cases, "tricks of the trade" that are not taught in school. A thorough exit and transition plan includes an ever-updated list of what needs to be transferred and how the transfer will take place.

Transitions take time, so detailed timetables should be in place for everything in the plan. Consider the difference between a plan that simply says the Healthcare Entrepreneur will move to part-time practice five years prior to retiring versus the plan that specifies a 20% annual reduction in hours worked each year for the five years prior to retirement. The odds of success are better for the latter plan.

> **TIP:** Although it can be argued that retirement planning is not the same as exit planning, it is recommended that Healthcare Entrepreneurs think long and hard about how they will spend their retirement and then field test their plans before they retire.

PROFESSIONAL WILLS

Healthcare Entrepreneurs keep track of changes in their profession. They position themselves so they can respond productively and in a timely manner to the changes that occur. Sometimes these changes are global, as when a new law comes into effect. Other changes are widespread, as when a new competitor enters the local market. Still other changes are far more focal, as is the case when disability or death strikes. None of us are immune to the possibility of untimely death or disability. Few of us want to take a good hard look at what would happen in the case of our own death or disability. But, doing so is a necessity. Failure to do so can leave your patients, your employees, and your family at risk.

Unfortunately, some of your professional responsibilities and the associated liabilities persist even after you die. Failure to meet these responsibilities brings the potential for negative consequences for your estate. Professional wills are the instructions you can leave for the management of your professional affairs in the event of your death or incapacity. Professional wills do not replace your personal will, which addresses the management of personal assets and other aspects of your affairs away from the office. Instead, professional wills guide the management of your professional responsibilities when you are unable to take those responsibilities yourself. You should have both types of wills.

Like any will, the professional will should include an Executor who has agreed to be responsible for implementing the terms of the will. It is wise to have at least one back-up Executor who will step in should the first Executor be unable or unwilling to do so. In some cases, the executor is paid a fee, but no payment is required. Since most healthcare professionals have unique rules and laws to follow, it is helpful to have an Executor who is either a member of your profession or who has access to someone who will consult with them to help them comply with your profession's ethics, norms, requirements, and mores. Like any document designed to ensure legal compliance, the professional will should be drafted by an Attorney.

Professional wills must address a number of key points and may address other points that are unique to your practice or of personal importance to you. For example, your will should address how the Executor can promptly notify patients that you will be unavailable. The will should also specify the options in place to ensure a smooth transition of care, including access to needed medications that may be in short supply. For legal and ethical reasons, it is important to have people and systems in place to protect each patient's clinical records and ensure that those records are available to the patient or their designee.

Your Executor may need to be HIPAA trained with a Business Associates Agreement signed well before they are called into service. As part of your written terms of service, patients can be asked to approve the release of information to your Executor in the event of your death or disability.

The will should also address how employees and vendors will be paid. When a practice is incorporated, the corporation continues even when its sole owner passes away. Since bills must be paid, revenues for services already rendered must be collected to cover the expenses. Steps should be prescribed to prevent new bills and new financial obligations unless there will be a flow of revenues with which to pay them.

In all likelihood, your licensing board and professional liability insurance carriers require that they are promptly notified of significant life changes such as death or disability. The professional will should list each of these required notices along with the appropriate account numbers and contact information for the recipients.

Sometimes, there are documents, obligations, passwords, and other things of value known only to one person. Sometimes such things are impossible for anyone to guess, such as your responses to questions computer programs ask to confirm your identity. Sometimes, they are more commonplace, as is the case with keys and contracts. For this reason, it is essential to inventory everything that you and you alone know about. Then, make sure that your professional will serves to pass that information along to your Executor.

SELLING YOUR BUSINESS

Ideally, as a Healthcare Entrepreneur, you will have faithfully followed the principles detailed in this book since the opening days of your practice. If, on the other hand, you have been managing your business on a catch-as-catch-can basis, the first step in preparing to sell a practice involves getting it into shape for sale. This is roughly analogous to preparing a home for sale. It may be tempting to try to sell "as is" to avoid the effort and expense of things like a new coat of paint or a repair to the long-broken handle on the pantry door, but failing to do so may ultimately cost you as the seller. As a seller, you want your practice to have curb appeal, with all systems in place and working well.

Asset Sales and Stock Sales

There are two primary categories of practice sales: asset sales and stock sales. An asset sale is likely to be the least lucrative. This involves the buyer purchasing those items that would appear on a properly maintained balance sheet, including Accounts Receivable, equipment, furnishings, and fixtures. Asset sales have different tax implications and different implications for liability than do stock sales. So, consult CPAs and Attorneys before serious discussions of a sale or purchase get underway.

When it comes to an asset sale, the ultimate selling price is likely to fall somewhere between the assets' appraised value and the price the market will bear. Even if an honest appraisal of the replacement cost of a set of assets is, let us say, $500,000, your ability to truly collect that amount will depend on how many buyers are willing to pay that price.

Stock sales can be more desirable for both the buyer and the seller. In a stock sale, the buyer purchases some or all the available stock in the practice. This approach saves the buyer the time and money needed to start a practice from scratch. Upon completion of the sale, the buyer owns part or all the practice lock, stock, and barrel. The seller has "cashed out."

SWOT Analyses

Preparing for a stock sale requires you to show off your practice in financial and numeric terms. As with any sale, potential buyers will likely have concerns about perceived flaws in the deal. These perceptions and the associated objections must be addressed and overcome. Healthcare Entrepreneurs who are contemplating selling their business should avoid the temptation to start by estimating the company's dollar value. Instead, it is prudent to start by listing the strengths, weaknesses, opportunities, and threats associated with your business; this is known as a SWOT analysis (see Table 10).

TABLE 10. SWOT Analysis

STRENGTHS	WEAKNESSES
● Our strong positive reputation. ● Broad based, large cadre of consistent referrers. ● Loyal patients with <3% drop-out rate/year. ● Superior fee schedules due to negotiations.	● We are behind the times with social media. ● Our patients are aging (avg. age 60). ● Computers and equipment are old. ● Staff lacks computer skills.

OPPORTUNITIES	THREATS
● Attract younger patients when competing practice closes in June. ● Add a pain clinic for our aging patients. ● Add a satellite office in up-and-coming young professional's locale. ● Purchase building next door to capture predicted real estate market growth + expansion.	● Biggest local employers are incentifying employees to enroll in HMOs. ● Consumer price index is outpacing the growth of our fee schedules. ● Hospitals are out-recruiting us. ● State subsidies for indigent care are on the chopping block.

Do not limit yourself to just one swing at this analysis; come back to it a few times. Between sessions, keep notes as to what you forgot to include. Show your SWOT analysis to others who are familiar with your practice — employees and consultants will add more perspectives and considerations.

Next, do the same analysis, using the same process, but come at it from the seller's perspective. Ask friends and colleagues to pretend to be a potential buyer and perform their own SWOT analysis. Sellers, rightfully, tend to be picky and critical. They are looking for the flaws in a prospective purchase. Make sure you are objective in your appraisal. Do not give in to the temptation to minimize factors that potential buyers will notice. Likewise, avoid the temptation to minimize or ignore a factor just because you can explain it away. Buyers do not think in terms of excuses. When you identify a weakness or threat, address it.

Finally, make a list of talking points emphasizing the strengths and opportunities that you have listed in your SWOT analysis. This should be done in bullet-point format. The expanded explanations can be shared later if a prospective buyer asks about them.

Use the talking points to create an action plan by which you will address the weaknesses you have identified. Be sure to include time frames and assignments of responsibilities so that you can track your progress. Sometimes the cost of addressing a weakness or threat outweighs the damage that weakness or threat will do to your sale price. In such a case, you may choose not to address the problem. But remember, many buyers, intentionally or otherwise, are looking for reasons not to buy.

Valuing Your Practice

With SWOT analysis and talking points in hand, it is time to consider the value and asking price of your practice. One way to do this is to retain a CPA, Business Broker, or Business Consultant to conduct a formal valuation. These professionals often identify strengths and weaknesses in the practice that you have overlooked. In addition, professionally prepared valuations tend to be perceived as more credible than those prepared by the seller. This can make negotiations a bit easier with less haggling. Of course, the valuation services and their advantages come at the cost of a fee.

The primary value of the stock is determined by the profits the practice can generate. Many buyers estimate the value of a practice using a financial statistic known as EBDITA. EBDITA is an acronym for Earnings Before, Depreciation, Interest, Taxes, and Amortization. Despite some shortcomings, this statistic appeals to buyers because it speaks to the business's ability to generate cash.

Typically, EBDITA is multiplied by some factor to determine a practice's value. From the buyer's perspective, the factor will determine how long it will take to recapture their initial investment. If, for example, a factor of four is applied, in theory, all things being equal, it should take the buyer four years to recapture their investment and begin to generate profits.

> **TIP:** Since revenues, net profits, and EBDITA all fluctuate year over year, it is worth considering each base factor over a two- or three-year range before committing to an asking price or offering price.

The magnitude of the factor applied to EBDITA can be influenced by a number of considerations, some of which reduce rather than increase the actual sale price. For example, a practice that has experienced a diminishing number of new patients in recent years may not have the same value as a long-established practice that has relied strictly on its existing patient base to generate new business via word of mouth.

Practices can be sold by their owners without the expense of a Business Broker. This approach makes particular sense when the buyer is already employed by the practice and has already been identified. Alternatively, Business Brokers are available to perform the time-consuming tasks of identifying buyers, helping negotiate the sale, and solving problems that arise before the closing. Like most consultants, brokers bring the additional advantage of expertise in identifying buyers and closing sales. Regardless of whether you retain a broker or choose a sale by owner, as a prudent Healthcare Entrepreneur, you should consult with legal, accounting, and business consultants extensively throughout the process.

Once you have sold your practice, do not forget to go back through your personal will, tax plans, investments, and other key documents. Things have changed in your life. Some of these documents will need to be reconsidered and amended.

Future Directions

"The future is now" is more than just a movie quote. Many of the business, service delivery, and payment models that will dominate the healthcare industry in the future are already being tested. Driving the change from the traditional fee-for-service model is the motivation of third-party payers to reduce costs and shift risks and responsibilities to those who provide healthcare services.

Insurance has always been about risk management. In the earliest days of health insurance, the lines were reasonably clear: patients could mitigate losses due to healthcare costs by paying a premium to insurance companies, which would absorb all the agreed-upon risk. The patient had nothing to lose if they overutilized healthcare services. Some patients, perhaps in the service of "getting my money's worth," did exactly that. In response, the insurance industry created barriers and penalties such as copayments and deductibles, which were designed to discourage overutilization. Faced with copayments and deductibles, patients had some skin in the game and were motivated to think twice about how they spent their own healthcare dollars. This was the beginning of a process in which those who are paid to absorb risk — the insurers — began to shift the risks back to their customers without reducing profits.

The trend toward reducing the insurance company's risks continued on a slower trajectory for many years and picked up speed toward the end of the 20th century. To be sure, there were capitated plans and HMOs that shifted the risks toward the healthcare professionals throughout most of that century. It was not until 1965, when Medicare started, that the government became an invested player in the process of risk shifting. Faced with the rising costs of Medicare, the government actively embraced the private sector's goal of shifting costs and risk away from the insurer. Legislation and other pressures were brought to bear, and the era we now refer to as the era of healthcare reform took off.

To be clear, healthcare reform as a process has been going on in the United States at least since 1798, when President John Adams signed legislation creating the first pre-paid health plan for disabled mariners. The term "healthcare reform," as used here, refers to the more meteoric changes of this century that are reasonably predicted to continue well into the future. Most of these changes surround efforts to shift risk away from the insurers.

The major trends of the coming years will predictably result in three significant outcomes, which in turn, will flavor the entire healthcare delivery industry. These outcomes are:

1. The lines between the insurers and the professionals who render healthcare services will be blurred at a minimum, and more likely eradicated.
2. New service delivery models will continue to emerge and evolve, thus requiring Healthcare Entrepreneurs to be flexible and adaptable but also providing the savvy Healthcare Entrepreneur with new, likely quite lucrative opportunities.
3. Healthcare decisions ranging from what technology makes it to market to which brand of a medication can be prescribed will be increasingly driven by economic rather than scientific forces.

THE BLURRING OF LINES AND ROLES

Historically, the relationship between insurers and providers of healthcare services has been that of friendly competitors. The two groups competed for a share of the money spent on healthcare. All the while, everyone was motivated to keep the patient happy and healthy. The insurers did so because customer retention is essential for any business, and they wanted their customers to renew their policies. The healthcare professionals did so because doing so is at the essence of healthcare delivery. For the most part, the two groups respected each other's roles.

At least three important things changed in the waning years of the 20th century and the opening years of the 21st century.

1. The costs of healthcare have not gone down despite all the health care reform efforts.
2. Legislation and other government pressures have empowered and emboldened the financial sector of our economy in general and the insurance industry in particular, thus shifting control over health care decisions away from healthcare providers and more toward those with unabashed profit motives.
3. The insurance industry has outperformed the healthcare industry when it comes to public relations. Well-funded campaigns by insurance companies to win the loyalty of its customers have been successful. As a result, public trust has

shifted toward the insurers and, as with any triangular relationship, away from the healthcare professionals.

In the context of these changes, forces have been whittling away at the boundaries between the two industries to the point that, in many ways, they have begun to meld together. Arguably the most striking example is the direct rendering of services at clinics owned and run by the insurance companies or their subsidiaries. In this model, those who provide services work for those who pay for the services. In the frenzy to control rising healthcare costs, regulators are turning a blind eye toward the obviously misdirected financial incentives and the lack of checks and balances inherent in this model.

Seeing the increasing profitability in healthcare and knowing that regulators have allowed mergers between insurance companies and pharmacies that appear to violate the principles of anti-trust legislation, large retailers have now introduced healthcare services delivered in their retail facilities. At some point in time, these retailers will be motivated to own or otherwise merge with the insurers. In all reasonable likelihood, these entities will outcompete those healthcare professionals who have not adhered to the principles of Healthcare Entrepreneurial practice. On the other hand, savvy Healthcare Entrepreneurs who keep on top of the changes will find ways to profit independently or in collaboration with their competitors.

The boundaries between insurers and healthcare service providers are being diminished in other ways as well. Managed care organizations have promulgated "medical necessity criteria" and "provider manuals" that guide and set limits on clinical decisions. The insurance industry's position has been that these documents do not interfere with clinical care, nor do they constitute the practice of medicine; they simply delimit what will and will not be paid for by their policies.

Insurers go on to emphasize that patients can always avail themselves of any option they choose if they are willing to pay for it out of their own pockets. Any freshman student of the psychology of economics knows that most patients, in most circumstances, will not avail themselves of such an option. To the patient, paying for insurance and also paying for a procedure feels like a loss. Humans are a loss-aversive species. Prescribers of diagnostic and treatment procedures have learned to limit their recommendations to comport with the insurance company standards to avoid putting their patients into a double-bind. Therefore, over time, the provider manuals have become powerful forces, directing healthcare decisions at the individual patient level.

DELIVERY MODELS OF THE FUTURE

Faced with mounting healthcare costs, which are projected to continue to increase significantly, third-party payers are constantly on the lookout for alternative delivery models. The Centers for Medicare & Medicaid Services (CMS) established the Centers for Medicare & Medicaid Innovation (www.innovation.cms.gov) to promote the development and testing of new models of healthcare financing and delivery. Arguably the most profound paradigm shift is from paying for time spent and services delivered to paying on a Value-Based Payment (VBP) basis.

At first blush, it is hard to argue with the notion that quality and outcomes should be part of any reimbursement scheme. Logically, those Healthcare Entrepreneurs whose patients fare better than average, and those who achieve desirable outcomes more efficiently, should be rewarded more than their colleagues. However, as with most things, the devil is in the details and the definitions of "value." Whoever defines criteria such as "value" will wield great influence over the entire healthcare industry.

If the best possible clinical outcome were the only factor used to determine "best practices," then science and outcome data would define those practices. However, other factors, such as cost per case and cumulative impact on national healthcare costs, are also taken into account by those who define "best practices." So, for example, routine tests such as annual blood work, cardiac stress tests, and PSA assays to detect prostate cancer, each of which has been proven to save lives, are ordered less often because they have been deemed not medically necessary.

The gap between what science says saves lives and what policymakers say is not medically necessary is due largely to where one draws the line in terms of cost-benefit.

A Word About Single-Payer System (SPS)

Many countries have government-run systems in which healthcare is universally available for all citizens. The option of adopting such a system in the United States has been the subject of hot debates since President Harry Truman began promoting it in 1947. The U.S. government is already responsible for a sizeable portion of the collective healthcare bill due to Medicare, Medicaid, and other government-funded programs. So, despite vehement opposition, the possibility of "universal healthcare" paid for by taxes and administered by the government remains a real possibility with supporting legislation being proposed at both the state and national levels.

Predictably, the insurance industry has lobbied legislators heavily to protect its business from government intrusion. The experience of the Veterans Administration (VA) suggests one possible way that the interests of the insurance industry can be reconciled with those of the proponents of a single-payer system. Specifically, when faced with more patient demand than it could handle, the VA did not simply refer their overload to the community at large. Doing so would have been a step toward creating a public-private partnership with the Healthcare Entrepreneurs who accepted such referrals. There would have been no need for insurers in such a system.

Instead, a triangular system that included room for big businesses was created. The VA contracted with a few entities that serve a managed-care role. These companies are paid to manage the cases referred to them by the VA and assign those cases to Healthcare Entrepreneurs in the community. So, even though the VA is essentially a single-payer system, room was carved in so that the big business and insurance functions remained a part of the system. This example may foreshadow how a nationwide single-payer system will be structured if such a system is ever initiated.

CPSIA information can be obtained
at www.ICGtesting.com
Printed in the USA
BVHW082045310821
615167BV00003BA/10